D1559144

ARGUMENTS OVER MUSEUMS AND HISTORIC SITES

VISITING
HISTORY

BY GERALD GEORGE

American Association of Museums

Published in 1990 by the American Association of Museums, 1225 Eye
St. N.W., Suite 200, Washington, D.C. 20005.

The chapter headings and text of this book were composed in New
Caledonia, a modification of the early 19th century typeface Scotch.
New Caledonia was designed by D.W. Dwiggins and became part of
the Mergenthaler Type Collection in 1938.

Publishing Coordinator: Evan Roth
Production Manager: Elizabeth Berland
Designer: McEver Design
Cover Photo: Philip B. George

With love, to Patti, Brian, and Roxane
—and to the great staff of AASLH, 1978-1987

ACKNOWLEDGEMENTS

I am grateful for encouragement and advice from several friends and colleagues who reviewed all or portions of this book in draft, particularly G. Rollie Adams, William J. Tramposch, Timothy C. Jacobson, Bob and Peggy Sanders, John and Kathleen Harkey, Judith Austin, and my history-minded brothers, Gene and Philip George. I also thank my former secretary, Ruth Kennedy, who has put more variations of this material through her typewriter than either she or I care to remember, and Kate Kelly, who did the copy editing. I am grateful to Edward H. Able Jr. and his fine staff for making it a pleasure to publish with the American Association of Museums. I am also grateful to many past and present members, officers, and staff of the American Association for State and Local History, who throughout my fourteen years there, shared so much with me, as thoughtful colleagues, editors, and friends.

—Gerald George

TABLE OF CONTENTS

Part III: History: Points of View

INTRODUCTION

THIS BOOK IS FOR PEOPLE WHO ARE DRAWN TO HIS-
toric sites and museums, to preserve them, to work in them, and to
visit them. Every day, thousands of Americans descend on Colonial
Williamsburg, the Gettysburg Battlefield, the Smithsonian's National
Museum of American History, old Fort Laramie, the USS Arizona
Memorial, and local history societies, eager to see something really historical. This book is about the problems involved in giving them "real
history."

Not the technical problems. Museum professionals already have an
impressive body of literature on how to make exhibits, how to give
tours, how to preserve buildings and conserve artifacts, even how to attract the public. But the public rarely gets a glimpse behind the scenes,
where museum professionals argue over what things to preserve and
what to tell visitors about them. This book is about arguments over historical significance—arguments about the meaning of historic sites and
museum collections and about the value of putting so much time, energy, and money into saving "our heritage."

These questions matter because in recent years we have been saving
things with unprecedented activism. The American Association for
State and Local History, whose members run museums, archives, historic sites, historic preservation groups, and historical societies, periodically publishes a directory of such historical organizations in the United States and Canada. The list has mushroomed from 904 in the 1944
edition to 9,375 in the 1986 edition—ten times the number of less than
50 years ago, and on the average a new one every two days. The 1990
edition of the *Official Museum Directory*, published by the American
Association of Museums, lists more than 6,700 museums alone, far

i

more than half of which have history collections. A veritable industry of curators, interpreters, preservationists, and related professionals, supported by thousands of citizen volunteers, has arisen to supply the modern mania for things historical.

Questions about this phenomenon matter also because history in our time is a theater of war. In 1988 the battle of "Third Manassas" broke out—a struggle between preservationists and a developer who wanted to put a shopping center on ground where General Lee once head-quartered, directly across from the part of the Manassas Civil War Battlefield that the U.S. Park Service already had preserved. Arguments between developers and preservationists over what is historically sacrosanct and what is not have become almost daily occurrences. Disputes over the historical significance of something are arguments over current value: How much of the past is worth bringing with us? Viewed that way, fights over historic sites become as real and as meaningful as any other battle for territory.

This book deals with many kinds of disputed significance. It contains essays I wrote—many of them dramatizations of issues—as I watched the battles unfold during my fourteen years on the staff of the American Association for State and Local History, nine as its director. I have attempted to tackle issues with humor as well as with sympathy, but each essay deals with a serious question.

The first section poses questions about history museums. In three essays I ask the following questions: What purpose do history museums have, given all the demands currently made on them? Must they be as frustrating as some of the slick new ones sometimes seem? Are they part of something larger that is happening to our society as a whole?

Questions in the second section arise from specific historic sites. From Drayton Hall: Why should we return a historic house to its "original" state? From Abraham Lincoln's birthplace: Why do we enshrine a log hut? From Old World Wisconsin: Does history "happen" only to the remote and great? From Cairo, Illinois: What really is "at the center" in the history of American cities? From various sites in northeastern cities: Do we present history accurately anywhere? From various sites in Wyoming: Why do we think history occurs in particular places? From the Bozeman Trail and Fort Phil Kearny: Are there historic sites with which we should not tamper at all?

Essays in the third section deal with what we preservers of history think it is. Successively: Can small historical societies treat history honestly? Is state history worth studying? Are there sensible ways to celebrate historical anniversaries? Are university professors the only serious historians? And finally, is American history, as most of us have learned it, more than a great story, a magnificent myth?

Such answers as I offer are not always directly stated or unwaveringly held, but I am certain of this: In the history-visiting business, we have not yet argued about fundamentals enough. In what follows I hope to be provocative enough to help.

PART I
Issues in Museums

WHAT HAVE YOU DONE WITH THE MUMMY, DADDY?!
OR HARWELL FACES ROCKS

THIS IS THE STORY OF WHAT IT CAN BE LIKE TO BE director of a small history museum in our time. The story—the melodrama—begins with some facts. The following item appeared in the newsletter of a state historical society:

> Three pickup truck loads of rocks, collected by Mr. and Mrs. C.H., were given last summer to the Pioneer Museum. Former residents of the county, the H's collected the rocks the past 20 years. The collection, in milk cartons, cardboard boxes, sacks, and containers of all kinds, includes fossils, feldspar, petrified wood, agate, and several kinds of quartz.

Let us pretend that we are there when those three truck loads of rocks are being delivered. It is early morning, a nice bright morning, bright enough to make the quartz sparkle. In the office of the Pioneer Museum is its director, Harwell Houdini, who got the job in part because his name suggested the possession of necessary qualifications. He is slumping down in the chair behind his desk, contemplating the sundry containers already piled on and around it. The museum's combination janitor, carpenter, and handyman has just set down, on top of the desk, an armload of milk containers, heavily laden.

"Well, Mr. Houdini," the handyman remarks, "nice mess of rocks, eh?"

Harwell slumps down even farther. He replies to the handyman, "I don't suppose all of the feldspar is in the milk cartons, all of the quartz is in the coffee cans, all of the fossils are in the cracker boxes, all of the agates are in the tuna tins, and all of the petrified wood is in the polyethylene leaf sacks?"

"I don't know a agate from a longhorn cheese myself," the handyman allows, "but it looks to me that various kinds of things is pretty well jumbled together. You sure you want all these rocks here in your office?"

"There's nowhere else in the museum to put them," Harwell says. "The collections we have are already bursting out of the basement." He slumps even farther down in his chair.

Already, at first word of the trucks, Harwell had called his friend and sole museum colleague in the region, Chickasaw Charlie, operator of the snake ranch, wax museum, and curiosity shop at the edge of the town by the highway. Charlie annually nets twice what Harwell's salary would be if the museum ever raised enough money to pay it fully.

"Charlie? Possibly you have heard that we have come into a considerable bequest of rare and valuable rocks?" Harwell had tried.

"I'll give you $25 a pound for any agates," Charlie had responded, "and a nickel a stick for petrified wood. No substitutes. Top offer. You gotta deliver, of course."

Harwell is still trying to calculate how much that offer would come to when all of a sudden the room floods with light and an angelic being with a golden wand floats down from somewhere in the ceiling.

"Who. . .who are you?" Harwell asks.

"I am the Good Museum Fairy," the apparition replies.

"No kidding," Harwell says. "Pull up a rock and sit down."

"I'm not here to joke, Harwell," the Good Museum Fairy says. "I want to know what this bequest is going to do to all your dreams. Why have you accepted all these rocks?"

"I didn't," Harwell says. "The trustees did. They thought it was an unusual collection. They like it."

"But these rocks are from all over the world," she protests. "They don't have anything to do with here. They don't explain anything here. You can't use them to help people here understand and appreciate and enjoy life here. You can't even use them to help visitors find out what is interestingly different here. This isn't even a science museum."

"It is now," Harwell sighs. "Unless I can learn how to make a rock garden."

"Harwell," the fairy fusses, "you and your board don't have enough money now to carry out your official statement of purpose. How can you create new exhibits about the region, its physical character, its culture, and its history, and take care of all these rocks, too? And what about your hopes of developing a living history farm?"

But Harwell has no time to answer because someone else is knocking on the door. Poof! The Good Museum Fairy vanishes. In walks a smiling young man.

"Good morning. I hear you have received a bequest of fossils and petrified wood and the like," the young man says cheerily. "I wonder if by chance the collection includes any remains of Native Americans or any Native American artifacts from burial sites."

"I don't think so," Harwell says, not thinking at all. "But in the museum here, we do have a few Indian artifacts that we use to try to show what Indian life was once like in this region."

"Very interesting," the young man says. "I am a Native American myself and an attorney representing a group of federated tribes interested in protecting the remains of our ancestors. We would like to make an appointment to speak with you further, say in about fifteen minutes."

"Well, all right, sure," Harwell says. "See you in fifteen minutes."

Near the end of that interval, the handyman, leaving the pickup trucks, comes rushing into Harwell's office. He crawls through the tunnel he has left in the rocks so that Harwell can get in and out of the room. Peeking up at Harwell over the desk, he exclaims: "I think you better get out here fast! There's a whole passel of Indians outside, and they are saying you promised to come out and talk with them."

Harwell crawls through the tunnel and arrives outside. There, near the front porch of the museum, stands the attorney and several thousand Native Americans—men, women, and children, in both conventional and traditional garb. They look angry and sad at the same time. Right behind them are four television cameras and several dozen reporters.

"Sir," one of the television reporters fires off right away. "These people say that your exhibition of Indian relics is a desecration of things sacred to them, a sacrilege against their religious traditions, and shows a callous disregard for their humanity. What is your policy about this, sir?"

It dawns on Harwell that he doesn't have a policy; the issue hadn't come up before.

"We want the religious artifacts and the bones," the lawyer says.

"But. . .but," Harwell finally gets out something about the claims of science, and how the museum is trying to teach about the traditions of native people, and anyway, he couldn't give up a county possession without approval of the board of the museum.

"That's pretty weak," the lawyer says as the TV cameras spin out acres and acres of pictures of Harwell's open mouth and red face. "We're coming back at this time tomorrow. We advise you to have your board here with a better answer. We believe those relics rightfully belong to our people."

When they are gone, Harwell turns back into the museum. "What are you going to do, boss?" the handyman asks.

"I don't know for sure," Harwell replies. "Except, could you possibly finish unloading by bringing the rest of the rocks through the windows and piling them up against the front door from inside?"

Just as he finishes saying that, in through the door comes the Dismal Man. Harwell calls him that after a character in Charles Dickens's *The Pickwick Papers*, who tells long stories about people getting sick and dying and leaving their families without bread. The Dismal Man has been keeping a close eye on Harwell's plans for the living history farm.

"Hi, how's it going?" Harwell asks hopefully.

"Depressingly," the Dismal Man says. "I hear you are going to put a rock garden in the living history farm."

"I've thought of it," Harwell admits. "Why?"

"Do you have evidence that there were rock gardens of agates and feldspar and quartz on farms in this region historically?"

"Well, no, at least not yet," Harwell responds.

"Another thing," says the Dismal Man.

"What's that?" Harwell asks.

"There's no animal dung on the front yard of the farmhouse you are restoring."

"No," says Harwell, "I don't suppose there is. That's because we don't want anybody to step in it. Also, it doesn't smell good. We don't want to put off the visitors."

"Yes," says the Dismal Man. "That's the problem with the whole version of history you are going to present here. It will be all cleaned up. Nobody will be dying of cholera in the farmhouse. No farmer will be beating his wife. Everything will be neat and nice, and everyone who comes here will feel nostalgic for the good old days that never really were. You are going to romanticize history and falsify it."

"But people don't want to travel across half the county on Saturday and pay even our fifty-cent, bare-maintenance admission charge to see cholera and wife-beating and filth," Harwell says.

"The Smithsonian, I hear, is going to restore a slum," the Dismal Man says. "The least you can do is spread some dung on the front lawn." Then the Dismal Man stomps away, muttering, "Disneyland—it's going to be just another Disneyland."

Harwell has little time to reflect on that, however. The telephone is ringing and he has to crawl back through the rock tunnel to his desk to answer it. It is the program officer of a private foundation in the state capital.

"I am sorry to have to inform you," says the program officer, "that we have not been able to approve your application for a grant. But we want you to know that you are welcome to apply again next year."

"Fine," Harwell says diplomatically. "What will make my application any better next year?"

"We know your museum is still relatively new," the program officer responds, "but it would help if you were accredited by the American Association of Museums."

"Great," Harwell says. "We very much want to do that. Where do I get a grant to do the things we need to do to get accredited?"

"I don't know," the program officer says. "That does not fall within any of our grant categories."

"Do you have a category for rocks?" asks Harwell.

There is no answer, but anyway, Harwell has to say goodbye because his other line is ringing. This call is from Washington, from a program officer at the National Endowment for the Humanities.

"We have just heard that you have come into a new collection at your humanistic museum," this caller says, "and therefore we urge you to apply for one of our challenge grants. Probably you will need to undertake a capital gift campaign to house your new collection, and a challenge grant can be the beginning of it. Also, we need applications in that category. Can you help us out?"

"Sure," Harwell says. "You want to just send a truck with the money, or what?"

"No," says the program officer. "You need to apply, and then you need to match the grant three dollars to one."

"Oh," Harwell rejoins. "Well, will you take quartz and feldspar as part of the match?"

Ignoring that, the program officer says: "While you are at it, would you please apply for a grant to do something in your museum with social history. The Congress and our council want us to put money this year into social history."

"What is social history?" Harwell asks.

"Basically, it is the history of ordinary people, women, and ethnic groups. Maybe you could do an exhibit about ordinary people, women, and ethnic groups in your area."

"Maybe we could," says Harwell.

"Apply quickly," urges the program officer. "New Humanities Council members are being appointed who may not be as interested as the last ones were in ordinary people, women, and ethnic groups. By this time next year, we may be back to the old themes—great men, great events, and great books."

"Maybe I will apply for one of each," Harwell says. "Right now I'm up to my back pockets in rocks, but I'll let you know."

As he hangs up, he finds himself confronted by someone who has dug himself in. It is a teacher from the high school who looks very happy.

"Good morning," Harwell says. "What's with you?"

"I have discovered museums!" the teacher exclaims.

"Way to go," Harwell acknowledges.

"Listen," the teacher instructs, "it dawned on me last night why the kids get bored with history. It's because in class we just read out of a big, fat textbook about Herbert Hoover, the Gold Standard, and the War of 1812, right? None of that means anything to the kids here. That history seems away off in Washington or somewhere. So I want them to do some local story to get the idea that history is real. I want them to go up in their attics and find stuff about what mom and dad did in the Depression. I want them to go to the old folks home and make oral history recordings. I want them to go down to the county courthouse and make copies of election returns and deeds. And then I want them to come to your museum and give you all that stuff for safekeeping and also see your exhibits—the tangible artifacts that make history real! And you'll have two or three people ready to show them around and explain everything, right?"

"Right," Harwell says. "And if they come right now they can help me move quite a few rocks. Who is going to pay for these 'two or three people' and all?"

The teacher looks shocked. "But, that's your purpose, isn't it—to put the young in touch with the old, to provide education, to help us teachers teach?"

"That's part of it," Harwell sighs.

"Good!" the teacher exclaims with satisfaction. "I'll start tomorrow. I'll send thirty kids per hour over here for five hours, and you take it from there."

Then the teacher rushes out with glee.

In his wake, a history professor from the local college appears through the tunnel in the rocks.

"Aha!" she exclaims when she sees Harwell. "I've got you now. I just heard you didn't get any grants this year again, which I suppose means that you still aren't going to help me with my research."

"You could take up geology," Harwell offers.

"Nonsense," she replies. "This is a history museum and you need to get with it. Surprise! I got a grant myself! A grant from the Humanities Endowment in Washington, D.C., to do research on local social history! Now then, I will need local records and local artifacts, particularly about ordinary people, women, and ethnic groups, and how plain folks around here lived and worked and played and worshipped and voted and all that. So, you better come up with some material culture and other local history stuff for me to study."

"Rocks have been very big in social history," Harwell suggests

"Don't put me off," warns the history professor. "If you don't exist to serve scholarship, what do you exist for?"

The history professor looks as if she may pick up a piece of rock and throw it. Ducking, Harwell responds, "I am beginning to wonder if I know."

That evening, Harwell crawls through the rocks, leaves the museum through a window so as not to unblock the door, and drives home. There he is greeted by his daughter.

"Daddy?" she says.

"Yes, dear?" he replies.

"The teacher brought some of us kids to the museum this afternoon. There were a lot of rocks there, but I didn't see you. I also didn't see something else. Daddy, I know pioneers and rocks and stuff like that are important but. . .but. . .Daddy, what did you do with the old Egyptian mummy? That's what the kids always like best? I hope you didn't give it away!"

"Yes, dear," he has to confess. "I'm afraid I did. It didn't really have anything to do with our community, and, well, we need more money. So I sold it to Chickasaw Charlie. It will fit into his place very well. But if you like, I'll take you there to see it on Saturday. It will cost us only twelve dollars each to get in."

Harwell then turns in for the night, hoping that by morning all this will seem just a silly story. A lot of museum directors these days wish it were.

THE BEST LAID PLANS OF MICE AND MUSEUMS: OBSERVATIONS ON GOING ASTRAY

THIS IS ABOUT A MUSEUM I ENCOUNTERED IN A dream. A general museum, its purpose was to explain the natural, cultural, and historical character of its region in the West. What a fine new building it had in which to do that. The architects designed it without windows to maintain strict climate control inside and protect the fragile artifacts. But they made it human in scale, attractive, indeed inviting. I judged from its proportions that the planners had allowed ample space for storage, exhibit preparation, conservation facilities, and all the other "backstage" requirements of a modern museum. I walked up the wheelchair ramp, dropped my four dollars in the glass box marked "Suggested Contribution $4," accepted a colorful brochure with a floor plan from the smiling receptionist, and found my attention immediately captured by the sight of a great stuffed buffalo.

Behind the shaggy creature rose a blown-up photograph, a huge montage showing more buffalo, as well as cattle, a wide-open range and an oil refinery, a covered wagon and a streaking jet. Arching over that artistic array appeared a handsomely lettered legend: "The Winning of the West." Yes, they had planned well: Catch the interest of the average visitor—most likely, like me, a devotee of "Gunsmoke," Zane Grey, and John Wayne westerns. Draw him or her by the eye into part one of the permanent exhibits. I succumbed readily, indeed cheerfully, as if a willing follower in the herd of that old buffalo.

Inside, another large sign immediately accosted me: "The First Westerners." I understood; this was, so to speak, chapter one, "Indians." One appeared, in fact—a mannequin, his look intense, his arm back, ready to hurl what looked like a real spear toward a woolly mammoth, painted in the distance in a life-size diorama. The mammoth was

11

caught knee-deep in a kind of bog, attacked by several spear-throwers. So that's how they did it, I said to myself.

Then I set out along an aisle where well-lighted exhibit cases showed me aspects of the aboriginal fellow's life, somewhere in the few million years between the advent of humanity and what his descendants might consider the Columbian calamity of 1492. Subheads introduced each topic: "Tools for Survival," "The Shaping of Stone," "Weavers and Potters," "Spirit and Ceremony." Then there was a place to sit down. Good timing, good planning!

Across from the seat I noticed a button to push. It produced on a little screen a video program about the excavation of a dinosaur pit. It began:

> "Long before the coming of even the earliest man. . . ."

This program was a sidebar of sorts, between the chapter covering unrecorded time and the chapter on the beginnings of history. Very thoughtful, very nice. So why did I feel guilty backtracking, after the video, to stare again for a while at one ceramic effigy that had held my attention more than long enough to read the label under it—an incredibly expressive head? This moves me, I thought, the way so called "primitive art" once moved Picasso and Modigliani. But actually, the label explained, the pieces in this case illustrated only an advance in the technology of making clay pots.

Well, time to move along, anyway. A whole new chapter awaited me: "From Pathfinder to Pioneer." (Wonderful alliteration!) A well-planned turning of the page, this sign appeared in a dramatically open area as one emerged from the low-ceilinged, prehistoric tunnel. Here began truly a new era—the appearance of Europeans. A big map with variously colored lines and arrows illustrated exploration. In this chapter, subheads soon appeared over attractive exhibit cases about the French *coureurs de bois*, the English of the Hudson's Bay Company, the American "mountain men." The cases held gleaming swords, shining muskets, bright-colored powderhorns. Originals, I supposed.

Nearby in a corner stood Jim Bridger, the mountain man turned frontier scout, who sooner or later went everywhere in the Rocky Mountains. His mannequin, wearing buckskin and holding a beaver pelt and a metal trap, knelt beside an ersatz stream "running" between tree trunks that looked as if they might be made of genuine wood.

Turning the corner, which was the only way past Bridger's craggy countenance, I suddenly saw "Settlement!" A sign said that. Here appeared a cutaway cabin in which I could view rude domestic utensils. A wagon with harness stood next to a blacksmith's anvil. Then the centerpiece—a long wooden trough with real water pouring through it, a sluice mine actually operating there in the museum! I sat down before it. I tried to figure out where the water came from. I listened to the lull of it. I fell asleep.

Not for long, though. The museum obviously planned this as a tarrying point for visitors, but only to refresh us for resuming once again the "trail." Now it narrowed past cases of mining pans, trading post wares, and ranch equipment. Designers had engulfed the artifacts in blown-up photographs and labels, with type size inversely proportional to the sophistication of their information. Beautiful creations, these exhibit cases; ought to be in an art museum, I kept thinking. Suddenly—here was an art museum.

That is, here was a gallery, containing the museum's collection of landscape paintings. I could tell it was an art gallery because the labels said only what art museum labels typically say, such as, "Scene on the Yellowstone, R.D. Eisenkratz, 1834-1902." Apparently this was a planned aesthetic interlude in the great sweep of the region's history. Some of the paintings even seemed impressive as paintings. I wondered. . . . But then I wandered too close to the next exhibit area, which irresistibly caught my eye.

It offered Nature. That's inspired, I thought, to link the landscape in art to natural science. Here the subheads differentiated geology, animals, plants. In this alcove, I found natural settings depicting differences in the region's stratigraphy and climate: a stuffed bighorn sheep in a mountain backdrop above the cedars and pines; a stuffed mule deer down closer in the foothills along streams bordered by aspen and cottonwood; two stuffed antelope out in the prairie grass of the treeless, open plain. Then I entered a dark little room, where fluorescent light made the region's ore-rocks and gemstones sparkle within glass cases. Back outside, big panels of drawings showed the effects of glaciation, "hot-spot" eruptions, and tectonic plate shifts on the thrusting up and wearing down of mountains in the region. Announced the concluding panel: "There is more oil in the oil shale that covers much of the western U.S. than there ever was under the sands of Arabia."

Before I could contemplate that, however—bang!—I was back on the historical trail, in a new era. How did I get there? Again the planners successfully grabbed me with another irresistible sign. "Clash of Cultures," this new chapter heading proclaimed, right at the entrance to the next exhibit section.

There in an open area, the Indian wars received elucidation. A big map pinpointed the region's major engagements. Cases on one side exhibited mocassins and headdresses, leather shields and feathered arrows, tomahawks and peacepipes, all next to labels and drawings and photographs describing the region's tribes and their ways of life. Cases on the other side described white military campaigning, exhibiting canteens and hardtack, blue suits and bugles, epaulettes and service revolvers, all amid pictures of Army life. In the center, two mannequins locked arms in combat, showing the intended use of real martial artifacts. One combatant appeared to be a uniformed relative of Jim Bridger; the other was out of the same mold as the figure I had seen felling the mammoth near the front of the exhibit hall. Above, a painted mural presented more fully the story of the battle that had opened the territory to white settlement.

How interesting, I thought, sitting down. I discovered in so doing that, at just the moment I wanted more detail, there was another screen and button. I pushed it. A theme from Dvorak's "New World" Symphony sounded as I saw a peaceful scene of meadows. A voice much like the earlier one began:

> "Long had the Indians followed the buffalo into this
> land of plenty. . . ."

Five minutes later, I had the whole picture, embellished by the sounds of creaking wagons, war chants, and the clatter of firing rifles. After establishing in some detail the exact movements of the antagonists on the final battlefield, the film concluded that the numerically and technologically superior culture won. Nice, I thought; one can hardly quarrel with that.

"More exhibits," directed a sign hanging at that room's only exit. Dutifully I went around another bend, created by cleverly arranged exhibit cases, until I found myself in the next "chapter," "The Rise of Settled

Cities." Here the museum's gun collection appeared within a recreated storefront that illustrated late-19th-century commercial architecture; cleverly the planners had killed two birds in one space, I thought. Here also was the Victorian parlor period room, without which no modern museum is complete, just as no self-respecting museum of an earlier era would have been without an Egyptian mummy or a two-headed calf. How elegant the furniture—it looked as if it had just come from some early equivalent of a department store. I guessed it was part of the plan that nothing in the history exhibits should look old. On I went, past the "subhead" exhibit cases, covering commerce, industry, education, and the railroad.

There the museum stopped.

How appropriate, I thought. The West had now been won. The land, its animals, and its original inhabitants had all been subjugated. Cities had arisen with the arrival of trains, poised and ready to carry progress to still another level. It seemed to me the story line was irrefutable, very much like the irresistible track of a fast freight. There at the end the gift shop beckoned, also, no doubt, planned. However, a big label did explain that exhibits had not yet been installed to bring the story of the region up to date. History was to be continued.

After I mailed the postcards I bought in the gift shop, I had lunch and thought about it all. On the one hand, I felt happy; I had just had a fascinatingly informative two hours in an admirably well-planned museum. On the other, I felt demeaned, as if I had been led by the nose through a canned presentation of slickly packaged pap. I felt I had been made to read a history textbook, illustrated with objects as well as photographs, all of which had been subordinated to a thin story line and selected for their conformity to it. It was a textbook ruled safe for school use by the state board of education's adoptions committee. Something was missing; something got left out of the otherwise splendid plan.

Uncertainly, I threw away the rest of my burger, walked from the restaurant back to the museum, and stuffed another four-dollar contribution into the glass box. What were the possibilities?

Well, for one, what if I tore out all the trappings—the photographic backdrops, the drawings, the labels—everything in fact that wasn't an artifact? Then it would be just me and the collections in their cases. The old cabinets of curiosities that museums used to have, however dull and uninformative, did allow the use of one's imagination. Suppose we could revive them in connection with computers. Suppose I could sit down in front of that fascinatingly expressive aboriginal ceramic and punch a button on a console at its case. (There would be plenty of room for seats now, by the way; I'd be able to sit down any time I wished.) The computer would give me a menu. If I punched "archaeology," the computer would tell me all about where the pot was found and how and by whom. If I punched "anthropology," the computer would tell me all about the culture of the people who made it. If I punched "technology," the computer would tell me about ceramics and how this pot was made and what it illustrated in the development of techniques of pot making. If I punched "art," the computer would tell me about the aesthetic qualities of such pieces, and maybe even show me other examples for contrast and comparison. If I felt like it, I could even punch nothing and just enjoy looking at the thing.

Imagine that, a whole museum full of nothing but objects—works of art, specimens from nature, historical artifacts—and computer screens. The collections would be supreme again, liberated from subordination as mere illustrations of story lines, and the museum would be organized to respond to visitors' questions, in ways controlled by visitors. Each artifact could "tell" twenty stories, not just illustrate one. Program variations could be added in future, including approaches we hadn't thought about yet. This wonderful house of treasure would become inexhaustible.

Wait a minute—that suggested another option. Having dismantled in my mind the first section, the archaeological exhibits, I now strode boldly into the era of European incursion and addressed the figure of the old frontier explorer, Jim Bridger. "Bridger," I yelled, "what do you know that's new? What research is under way in this place? Is anybody here adding to our knowledge of who first came to this region and why, of exactly where they went and what they did, of their cultural patterns, social structures, political systems, economic activities, and spiritual values, of the meaning of their material culture? What are you looking for in this museum? Clue me in to what you are trying to find out? Instead of just squatting there in that silly suit—explore something!"

Next I barged on into the mini-art gallery that held the regional landscape paintings. First I stood in the middle and let my eye rove around at them. I picked out one to inspect more closely, then another, then another still, until, in an order of my own choosing, I had studied all of them. Then I took out my handkerchief, and tore it into three strips, which I labeled "first," "second," and "third." Then I placed each next to the paintings I decided deserved those rankings.

Perhaps it is not surprising that by now I had attracted attention. A curator, apparently on routine tour, demanded disapprovingly, "What are you doing?"

"I am judging these paintings," I replied. "This is an art show, right? No? I have misunderstood? You mean these paintings are part of the permanent collection? Oh, well then," I went on, encouraged by his puzzled stare, "are they here because of their value as pictorial documentation for this region? Then what do they depict and how accurate are they? Or are they here because they are outstanding works of art? Or are they here for some other reason? I don't mind just looking at them, if I have a clue."

Then I simply walked away as if what I had said made perfect sense to the person to whom I had said it. He seemed content enough to see me leave the room, and did not at first follow. But he reappeared quickly enough when he heard the noise I made in rearranging the mannequins in the "clash of cultures" exhibit. I put the Indian on his back on the floor and stood the blue-coated soldier over him with his plastic foot on the Indian's chest.

"Hey, you can't do that!" the curator exclaimed.

"But don't you think this is more accurate?" I asked. "Beyond being a clash of cultures, it actually was the destruction of one by the other, was it not? No? All right, how would you arrange the figures? How do you see the long-term outcome? Could we at least raise a question or two in here?"

"If you don't leave," growled the curator, "I will have to have you arrested for destruction of property."

"No, no," I said, seizing the soldier's gun. "It is I who should arrest you for destruction. Those exhibits in the natural history section—you've stuffed a bighorn sheep to put in there. The bighorn sheep is an endangered species. Why don't any of your signs say anything about that? I'll let you off if you'll campaign to save bighorn sheep. Also, what in the world is the meaning of that label about there being more oil in the West's shale than under Saudi Arabia? Is that an argument for strip-mining? Or is that a commentary on the economics of oil production? Or a warning of a coming environmental issue? Or what? You can't just stick up something noncommital like that."

Ah, but this was indeed a well-planned museum. I had no more uttered those words than I found myself surrounded by security guards. Some remote buzzer probably went off when I moved the mannequins, or some camera transmitting to the security control center had shown me grabbing the gun. I found myself relieved of that. Then they hauled me out past the exhibits on the rise of cities, of commerce, of industry, of education.

"Hey, friends, I was just kidding," I protested. "I've merely been trying to imagine ways to get more life in this place, to make visitors respond to it. In these exhibits here, for example, what if you focused on the decision points in the region's development, the choices that made a difference? What if. . . ." Well, I had a lot of time in jail that night to think about it.

So, what is the point? Just that the museum I have described is a composite of several I have seen that have been effectively canned, not planned, and a lot of new museum exhibits seem headed that way.

My fantasy about a museum full of computers available to provide endless insight about artifacts may be far-fetched, but some museums already do use computers to pose and answer questions at the visitor's command, and technological advances may open up many possibilities for museums that want both to stimulate visitor inquiries and to respond to them. My fantasizing about computers and so forth is less a proposal of specific solutions than it is a frustrated plea for transcending shallow didacticism with something that encourages thought, feeling, and a second look.

Also, why cannot museum staff members be encouraged to involve themselves more in discovery, using exhibits to share new perceptions with the public? Why cannot museums more deliberately acknowledge conflict and controversy, bumps on the path of progress that introduce real life into a story line? Isn't history partly the study of abandoned options—alternatives sometimes embodied or expressed in artifacts? Why shouldn't museums more often even crusade?

Continuously taking sides on current issues may not make sense for museums, not just because it risks trouble with sources of support but also because the result is likely to be superficial. But some science museums these days rescue beached whales, try to breed threatened pandas, and teach whooping cranes to survive in the wild. Some art museums mount exhibits to assert the importance of little known painters or the beauty of inadequately appreciated art forms or the aesthetic achievements of underestimated cultural groups. History museums, too, are trying to go beyond exhibits that simply mummify artifacts. But I do not think it is enough just to make exhibits visually jazzier and hang artifacts on surface-level story lines.

What if, particularly in planning a history museum, we did not ask, "What story do we want to tell?" What if, instead, we asked, "What questions do we want to raise? And how then can the museum involve its visitors—and itself—in the search for answers?"

THE VIEW FROM THE DUMP AT THE EDGE:
A THEORY OF MUSEUMS

I

I SUPPOSE I GOT EMOTIONALLY CARRIED AWAY. There they were, the out-of-town developer and his local legal counsel—Pontius Pilate and Judas, to my infuriated mind—explaining their case to the city's Zoning Board of Appeals. Of course they recognized the historic character of the three-block row of Victorian-era warehouses on the city's riverfront, once a bustling commercial district where steamboats unloaded cargoes of all kinds. Of course they respected the desire of historic preservation groups to maintain the character and scale of that row, where other developers were tastefully turning the old structures into restaurants, shops, and office space. As responsible developers, they had intended to do exactly the same with the 19th-century buildings they had bought on the middle block in the row. Could they help it that "street people" had broken in, had built fires inside the old tinderboxes to get warm and heat their cans of beans, and had inadvertently burned the buildings down? They still would have saved what was left of the smoking facades if preservation groups or the city had come up with the necessary money. So what if they, the developers, had demanded thousands of dollars within just thirty days? The city's own health and safety department had pressured the developers to bulldoze the charred walls as soon as possible lest they topple over on some innocent citizen.

Now, the developers simply wanted to erect a 23-story office tower where the old four-story structures had been. Couldn't the preservationists see that their architect's design would make the skyscraper unobtrusive in relation to the rest of the district? Besides, long ago, on the other side of the street, the telephone company had already erected a great windowless fortress in which to keep its computers comfortable; this new building wouldn't be any taller than that. So, would the zoning appeals board please approve the variance that would enable them to erect a high-rise in the old district? The historic row would actually benefit because the new tower would bring more people, spending more money, into it.

They said something like that; I have paraphrased standard developers' arguments. I was too angry to remember exactly what they said as I succeeded them at the witness table to help present to the board the preservationists' side. But somehow I refrained from asking why the building hadn't been broken into until it had sat undeveloped for months, and whether the developers had let it sit so long because the tenants on which they had gambled hadn't materialized, and whether they had been undercapitalized from the start. No, and I also didn't ask whether the rumor was true that the fire department had detected kerosene at the fire site, and whether street people commonly drank kerosene with their beans. No, and I didn't even ask how much they had collected from the insurance company, although I knew insurance rates went up thereafter on buildings elsewhere in the row. I didn't ask all that because I had no more proof to support my insinuations than apparently the insurance company had.

But I did ask this: If the developers considered the old four-story buildings potentially profitable when they bought them, why wouldn't buildings limited to four stories be financially profitable there now—reconstructions of the old buildings or new ones harmonious in architecture and scale? Why the need to stick a twenty-three-story sore thumb in the eye of the entire historic area? And what about the next developers who might apply to add nineteen stories of greed to four stories of modest commercial profitability? What would keep those developers from arguing that both the phone company and the developers of the burned-out site had received variances already, so why shouldn't they? At what point do variances make a mockery of the cityscape they vary from? If anybody proposed to intrude this way on, say, the fascinating old city center of Amsterdam, we would all be up in arms. So why sacrifice to short-term interests the long-term value of our own still-visible history?

Standard stuff, of course, and as usual it didn't sell. The board split on the issue, but approved the variance by one vote. In search of solace, I walked through the "new" part of downtown to the state museum, a few blocks away. ("All we wanted were three contiguous blocks of 'history' out of the whole city!" I kept exclaiming.) I noted on the way a few individual historic structures remaining even in this part of the city, impressive architectural achievements from the past that the city prized enough to keep on using—the exceptionally original state capitol, a fine antebellum church, the grandiose old train station, turned into a hotel. But they stood in isolation, increasingly overshadowed by new skyscrapers. Even the state museum was new; one had to seek history inside it.

There the state's history was, however, preserved for eternity—the relics of the pioneers and the politicians, the soldiers and the financiers, those who threw the Native Americans out and those who built the cities up. Then, alas, it struck me: What is the history of this state other than development, day-in day-out, onward and upward even to twenty-three stories? Downtown Amsterdam represents a 17th-century golden age that is over. This town is still on the upswing; it expects to rise forever. However unacquainted the zoning board might be with actual historical information, its members have our city's history in their blood; when they favor development, their actions are faithful to the city's past. I had been the one asking for a true variance—a departure from the pattern of continuous replacement of old with new that fidelity to the dominant strain in our heritage would demand. No wonder they didn't give it to me.

Alas, that was not the only depressed message I read into the museum that day. I began to see that it was almost as filled with buildings as the downtown streets: an aboriginal hogan, a part of a log cabin, a huge mill with a water wheel, an early tobacco barn, the shops of artisans, and even the reconstructed facades of 19th-century commercial buildings not radically different from those on the three-block row. At least it was nice to see our buildings saved somewhere. The town had put them here, of course, because it didn't want them outside anymore, where they were in the way. The more I thought about that, the more it seemed a commentary not only on the nature of our culture but on the role of museums.

II

OTHERS HAVE TAKEN THE ARGUMENT MUCH FURther. Sometime after my difficult day, I read Umberto Eco. Not *The Name of The Rose*, his famous novel; rather, a book of his essays that Harcourt, Brace, Jovanovich published in 1986. I was most particularly interested in the essay from which the book takes its title: *Travels in Hyperreality*. Eco lives in Milan, teaches at the University of Bologna, and specializes (so the dustcover says) in something called semiotics, which involves the study of signs or the language of signs.

"Hyperreality" is something he saw signs of in America at Disneyland, the Hearst Castle, the Museum of the City of New York, the Lyndon B. Johnson Library, the J. Paul Getty Museum, the Movieland Wax Museum, the Palace of Fine Arts, the Madonna Inn, Oral Roberts University, the San Diego Zoo, Marine World, Knott's Berry Farm, Old Tucson, and the Forest Lawn-Glendale Cemetery.

All, Eco asserts, are part of a great "falsification industry" that ironically feeds the American need for "the real thing" and more of it. We recreate reality to the nth degree, he says, through wax statues and "audio-animatronic" people, natural habitats for animals, period rooms containing costumes and furnishings, transplantations of European villas and famous interior spaces, copies of works of art, reconstructed cities. Even sites and scenes that have existed only in literature are faked to seem real in such places as Disney World. Why? Demand for the authentic fake is the "offspring of the unhappy awareness of a present without depth . . . compulsive imitation prevails where wealth has no history . . . where Good, Art, Fairytale, and History, unable to become flesh, must at least become plastic. . . . America wants to establish reassurance through imitation."

Tucked away further in jolly old Umberto's cheerful chamber of American cultural horrors, we find this: In our reconstructions of European ruins (such as the Roman villa in the Getty Museum), and our reproductions of European art (such as those we show or sell, in almost every conceivable medium, of Leonardo's "fading" *Last Supper*), Eco sees "the theme of the Last Beach, the apocalyptic philosophy that. . . Europe is declining into barbarism and something has to be saved." However,

> [I]t is the entrepreneurial colonization by the New World (of which J. Paul Getty's oil empire is part) that makes the Old World's condition critical. Just like the crocodile tears of the Roman patrician who reproduced the grandeurs of the very Greece

that his country had humiliated and reduced to a colony. And so
the Last Beach ideology develops its thirst for preservation of art
from an imperialistic efficiency, but at the same time it is the bad
conscience of this imperialistic efficiency, just as cultural anthropology is the bad conscience of the white man who thus pays his
debt to the destroyed primitive cultures.

Similarly, so Eco insists, the American "love of nature" that is "a constant of the most industrialized nation in the world" is "like a remorse;"
if animals want to survive, they, too, "must submit to the falsification industry" in zoos. History the same. Eco is struck by a museum period
room, a reconstructed 1906 drawing room in New York: "[A] private
home seventy years old is already archaeology; and this tells us a lot
about the ravenous consumption of the present and about the constant
'past-izing' process carried out by American civilization in its alternate
process of futuristic planning and nostalgic remorse."

Does Eco mean to apply this to museums generally? Is he right that
what we are "saving," through fabulously fake recreations or through
"past-izing" in museums, is what we are in the process of destroying, or
have destroyed, outside? That museums in all their variety are where
we pay homage, like the Walrus and the Carpenter, to what we have actually devoured? Are museums our trophy rooms, where we show off
what we have captured (art), conquered (anthropology), overcome (nature), and outgrown (history)?

III

COULD THAT UNAPPEALING NOTION EVEN EXPLAIN
the whole puzzling phenomenon of American museum growth? That
question occurred with particular force one morning when, driving to
work, I saw two signs I couldn't remember seeing before.

One appeared posted at the edge of a stretch of undeveloped property. There in a woods of sorts, so I had been told, had lived an elderly
man with means enough to ignore developers' offers for his land,
which now lay well within the booming city's residential extension. The
man had generously provided in his will for what the sign now an-

nounced: "Future Site of City Nature Center," to be administered by the city's science museum. I called a friend there who confirmed, yes, the museum had been given the property, and had accepted the terms of the bequest, namely, that it was to be used to provide the city a "green space," where urban children could come see, pet, and grasp the reality of common, domesticated animals: chickens, cows, sheep, horses, and hogs. The farmyards and barns that once provided that experience had long receded far beyond the city's limits.

The second unexpected sign I saw that morning was a bumper-sticker on a car ahead of me. We were stuck in a long line backed up behind a red light on a street that was growing daily more exasperating, thanks to the additional traffic that new industrial plants in the area seemed to be bringing to the city. New plants, I thought, where farms used to be. The bumper sticker said: "Be a Zoo Booster!" For enlightenment on this, I called my dentist. Many times, lying there in fear and trembling as he drilled a root canal through nerves that shots of pain killer hadn't completely deadened, I had heard him expound on the incredible fact that a city grown as large as ours did not provide its citizens with a zoo. "Yes," he acknowledged cheerily when I called him, "a group of us has organized at last to undertake the fundraising."

Again, the rationale seemed altruistic. City kids need contact with living creatures other than themselves to understand that the earth is a shared space, that nature offers more than watered lawns, weeds struggling through sidewalk cracks, an occasional tree of service to dogs, and ourselves. Like nature centers, zoos provide that perspective and extend its range to include the wild and exotic. They even preserve cranes, koala bears, and other species nearly extinguished by the cement and smog and industrial excrement of human encroachment. They are museums for the living, for creatures that in some places are as endangered as historic buildings may be.

The federal Institute of Museum Services, in fact, includes zoos, nature centers, and historic houses within its definition of museums, along with more traditional museums of science and art and history. So does the American Association of Museums in its museum accreditation program. And museums of all kinds have been on the increase in more cities than mine. Museum mania has gripped the entire country. A "universe survey" of museums conducted by IMS in the early 1980s showed there existed at least 4,600—half of them new since 1960. That means that in roughly two decades, from 1960 to publication of the survey, somebody started a museum on the average every three to four days. By 1990 the *Official Museum Directory* listed more than 6,700.

There is no reason to think that growth has fallen off since. Through the mid-1980s, at the American Association for State and Local History, my phone seemed to ring all the time with someone wanting assistance: "We've saved the old train station; how can we make a museum out of it?" Or, "I'm head of the centennial commission; we need help—we've decided to create a museum." Listings in the association's directory of historical organizations grew from under 6,000 in 1982 to more than 9,000 in 1986; many of the additions were museums.

Over a couple of drinks at the end of a museum conference or association meeting, one or another of us could always come up with plausible explanations for museum mushrooming. American GIs returned from Europe after the Second World War impressed with Old World Culture from visits to such ancient cities, museums, and historic sites as had managed to survive modern bombs and other wonders of obliterative efficiency. Didn't the conquering New World Power also have old things to be proud of? Moreover, increased leisure gave us time, more disposable income gave us means, and the automobile and airplane provided us quick access for enjoyment of our heritage.

Rising patriotism in the Cold War era gave further impetus to American history museums, with Colonial Williamsburg in a tri-cornered hat waving the flag at the head of the parade. Federal agencies came into being—the National Endowment for the Humanities and the National Endowment for the Arts in the 1960s, the Institute of Museum Services late in the 1970s, among others—to toss financial fagots on the fires of museum development. Also in the 1970s, the Bicentennial of the American Revolution induced every community in the country to consider an appropriate commemoration; many chose to create a museum. So many cities had created museums by the 1980s that other communities launched plans for them if only to keep up with the Jonesvilles. Economic retrenchments in the 1980s ironically gave further impetus—now cities must have museums to market themselves successfully in the increasingly ferocious competition for tourist trade and business relocations. Corporate executives want cultural attractions as well as cheap labor, low taxes, and abundant energy sources. This is a fair synopsis of three-martini insight into the last half-century's phenomenon of museum growth.

Some of us have been sobered by recognition (documented in Urban Institute studies) that growth in museums has corresponded to growth in cultural and social service organizations generally. At least in the 1960s and 1970s, they grew parallel to growth in government. The entire non-profit sector boomed with federal assistance, designed to bring about what President Lyndon B. Johnson used to call The Great Society. In light of that, there may be nothing special about museums' growth at all.

Still I wondered if that were the whole truth. Perhaps we do have more museums for the same reason that we have more orchestras and juvenile delinquency centers, because in the middle of the 20th century, starting with postwar prosperity, the nation has had more money to spend on such things. But does that really answer the question? In relation to all the things we have thought we needed or wanted, why have we spent the money on museums, too?

Pondering such matters, I gazed out my office window overlooking a log fort that represents the city's original settlement on the riverbank. The Works Progress Administration erected the fort during the Depression. (We do rebuild history, I observed, as well as demolish it.) Interpreters now use the fort to exhibit crafts and describe frontier life. No developer proposes to obliterate that fort in favor of "progress" in the use of such prime property. Unlike the genuinely historic, original buildings on the threatened warehouse row, the fort is protectively encapsulated as a museum. Why? Maybe because it is something we don't need anymore, except to show us how far we have come. And it is too big to put inside a regular museum.

Museum growth in the 20th century has corresponded not only to growth of government and other public service activities. It also has corresponded to an incredible rate of technological and environmental change. Even the newest technology is changing so rapidly that already we have computer museums and museums about air travel and space. If we like a building, a bird, a stage coach, or even an old toaster, why don't we keep it in use or in sight outside? Because it is either obsolete or in the way. Are museums, accordingly, a means of not giving up entirely what we once had prized, of holding on to something familiar lest we get lost in today's maelstrom, of keeping pace with the rate of obsolescence creation? Have we needed more museums faster because, faster and faster, we have been throwing more things—styles of art, old buildings, pre-industrial cultures, historically outmoded objects, even animals—away?

IV

STUDENTS OF HISTORY MAY BE LESS COMFORTABLE than semioticians with such generalizations. Anxiety about my questions made me feel the need to flee somewhere outside my office to think. Drive, I ordered myself, out of the city if necessary, somewhere not so obvious as a park, or so full of people.

South through town I went, even farther on the traffic-choked street than I had come the morning when I noticed the signs. I continued far beyond my own residence, out to what used to be the city's edge, which instead, I now discovered, had become still another shopping center ringed by apartments and condominiums. Beyond that lay even more residential developments, until I realized I could go no farther and get back in anything like the available time.

Suddenly, to the side, a street appeared with ordinary, unlandscaped trees at its edges. I spun around at the next intersection, backtracked to the side street, and followed it into—nothing. Amid the trees and shrubbery, only the paved street itself had intruded. Had a developer gone bust here before he could build houses? Or was this a tract waiting for a construction company to finish some other concrete-centered assignment? I had no idea, but this place suited my purpose. From where I parked, I could see far off through the trees almost to the heart of the city.

I speculated that at night this place probably became a much-patronized lovers' lane. But at the moment, I was alone with a discovery. In the gutters and on the curbsides all along this unfinished avenue, this eerie extension of urbanization, this unintentional but readily accessible "nature center," lay the most incredible array of junk—ordinary trash, faded newspapers, old magazines, bald tires, rusty toasters, cracked batteries, silent television sets (their great eyes staring unblinkingly out of the underbrush), even couches (vinyl), tables (Formica), and broken chairs. One could see where each car or pickup had come, found its clear spot along the road, and unloaded its little clump of expended civilization at development's temporary dead end.

As I surveyed the debris, only the lulling hum of traffic just visible in the distance disturbed the stillness, and only vegetable life appeared, nothing human or animal, no scavenger or even simple squirrel, at least not at that moment, in the daytime. This place, plain and simple, was an undesignated dump. I wondered then how many there were like it at the edge of our city, marking its outer encroachment zone. Was this outhouse of abandoned artifacts one of many constituting a lifeless fringe around the town? A vision came to me of millions of such piles of junk ringing all our expanding cities, pushed almost imperceptibly farther and farther out as cities grew, as urbanization advanced, the way boulders once were pushed ever outward into rings by the forward flow of the great glaciers in the ice age.

Suddenly then, people appeared in my picture—frantic curators, picking over the piles, trying to keep up as the urban glacier moved and the accumulations of discarded objects grew. Curators from museums trying to bear the salvage burden of an onrushing civilization's transformations. The fact that they were not really there did not mean it was not happening. Would they, could they, be fast enough to sort out and save the things of most significance?

Surely, it seemed to me then, the historic preservation movement and the museum movement parallel in their growth the world's general concern with ecology; surely they can be understood as branches of the effort to defend the environment as a whole. All are responses to forces that are transforming the planet at an ever-increasing rate. Museums are dumping grounds, yes. But they are also shelters. Whether they contain animals, art, or artifacts, they are attempts to preserve some remnant of past reality, to construct some sort of bridge from past to future over the present abyss, to ameliorate some of the destructive side effects of change. They are efforts to maintain at least the illusion that we still know who we are, and where we live, and can control what we are doing and where we are going.

The vision soon faded. I saw I was alone again with the trees, the trash, and the street. Something glittered at me in one of the little piles. I got out of my car, walked over, and picked it up. What do you know, I thought—an old wind-up clock, made out of metal! You don't see many of those anymore.

I returned to my car, started the engine, and drove slowly back to my office. I took the old alarm clock with me. I could use it for a paper-weight, I thought. And visitors would find it interesting, a curiosity to be touched and fiddled with. Who knows, I thought, I might even use it to keep track of time.

PART II
Exploring Historic Sites

THE GHOSTS OF DRAYTON HALL

DOES AN OLD BUILDING HAVE A HISTORY LOCKED
up in it waiting to be revealed, something it can be made to "tell?" That
mystical concept is part of the folkloristic tradition that makes us associate old houses with the haunts of ghosts. But sometimes even sophis-
ticated historians gain by trying to hear them. Let us go, for illustration,
to Drayton Hall.

Let us suppose that it is night as we set out for the stately old mansion. Unless developers have made "progress" in its vicinity even more
rapidly than I fear, we can still get there by an appropriately narrow
road through an appropriately dense border of trees, just a good buggy
ride upriver from the city of Charleston, South Carolina. Or we can
take the route by which many Charlestonians used to come; we can go
by rowboat up the Ashley River, preferably on a romantically moonlit
night. We can get off at the old landing and then approach the house
on its slight rise by a grand pathway that once ran through beautiful
gardens. The walk is short enough not to tire visitors but long enough
to give them time to be fully impressed with the gracious grandeur of
the house.

Nobody lives in Drayton Hall any more. Its windows will be dark
when we come because the last of the Draytons left in 1976, after one
of the most miraculous things about it—the fact that, generation after
generation, members of the same family occupied it for more than
two-and-a-quarter centuries. It belongs now to the National Trust for
Historic Preservation. Two other organizations took part in purchasing
and preserving it and have a voice in its affairs: the Historic Charleston
Foundation and the parks department of the state of South Carolina. A
staff of preservationists under one of the trust's professional site administrators maintains the site and provides tours.

On the night we come, however, let us not ask any of those authorities what the story of the mansion is. What the trust has done with the house so far—or more precisely, what the trust has not done—leaves its ghosts still free and unencumbered to tell us, if they will. The trust has disturbed the mansion only to the extent of stabilizing it—that is, of applying preservation treatments where necessary to prevent deterioration, but without restoring the property to the way it was in some former time or putting furnishings in the house. In the daytime, the trust's interpreters take small groups through the empty house, point out architectural features that could not be seen so easily if it were refurnished, and tell about its long and remarkable history. We are not used to using our imaginations at such sites; old mansions crammed with antique bedsteads and portraits and parlor chairs are more familiar. This property more than any other operated as a museum enables visitors to view a historic house unrestored, empty, and unadorned. Some of the ghosts, one might well imagine, do not like it.

Light a candle and listen, for example, to the shade of old John Drayton, who might be heard saying something such as this:

> "I am the grandson and son of Draytons who settled this area in colonial times, and I built this house between 1738 and 1742. I ran several plantations from here and rose to serve on the King's Council for South Carolina. I begat a line of physicians and lawyers and political leaders, including one who (after the unfortunate rebellion against England) became governor of the South Carolina state. I'll tell you what this house should be famous for—it embodies the glory of colonial South Carolina!
>
> "Its very design is monumental. See those columns, that two-story portico, the classical pediment, the double flight of steps, the connected structures symmetrically flanking the main house on both sides? Inside, see the ornamented ceilings, the rich cornices, the elaborate fireplaces, the great entrance hall? Did you ever see a home so grandly impressive in all your life? I built it here long before the Washingtons or any of those other subsequently more celebrated Virginians raised anything like it on their famed tidewater plantations. We South Carolinians need take no back seat historically to anyone, and that's how this house should be interpreted now, I tell you.
>
> "Take out those damned mistakes, those additions to the house and grounds that some of my misguided descendants made. That mound out in front of the house—a silly Victorian

rose garden. It ruins the symmetry of the lane that runs between the house and the front road. Get rid of those 19th century balustrades. They contradict the vertical thrust of the original design. That Victorian cottage, those ponds, that privy—move all those latter-day additions. They detract from my grand lawns and vistas. Replant my formal gardens, and refurnish the rooms of the mansion completely, so that all the world may recognize the mistake that historians have made in treating South Carolina as less accomplished than certain other American colonies."

How could that view from old John Drayton not provoke an exasperated challenge from the ghosts of his immediate descendants? They would rise at once to remind him how hard it had been to maintain the mansion through the era after the Revolutionary War. Why? Because of the debts he had run up to make the place glorious, and because he had refused to side with the patriots in the struggle. Those voices would subside only to let us hear still later Draytons, bitter in humiliation, who knew how close the house came to destruction in the American Civil War. Listen now as we light another candle:

"The glory of South Carolina, is that what you want? Then maybe you should show the house as it was in the War of Northern Aggression—exhibit it with sickbeds for furnishings and weeds in place of crops and gardens. We had to make it a hospital to keep the Union troops from burning it down. Let the Yankee tourists now come to enjoy the nostalgic pathos of 'Southern decadence,' Scarlet O'Hara and all. That's what those Washington administrators who finally did get the place away from us are doing by just leaving it bare. National Trust for Historic Preservation? Just more carpetbaggers."

But behind those voices rise others more strident from still another Drayton generation:

"We're not interested in colonial or antebellum glory, or romanticized suffering either. Remember this—we later Draytons did save this house; we did restore its prosperity and grandeur. Phosphate mining may not seem high class to colonial aristocrats or decayed gentility, but it enabled us to maintain the old mansion for another two or three generations, well into the 20th century.
"Profits from the phosphate we discovered on the Drayton property also enabled us to make renovations in accord with our own taste. We like the mounded rose garden. We also like the

balustrades, which not only were elegant additions but kept our kids from falling off the upper story porches. We earned the right to make things grand again in our own way, and if you change everything back to the way it was in the 1740s, you'll obliterate the evidence of our equally glorious era in the old property's history. If anything is restored, it ought to be the furnishings from our time. They were beautiful, and (it's about time some of you older Draytons listened to us practical ones!) such furnishings, or items like them from the Victorian period, may still be around somewhere. Colonial antiques are scarce and costly, but you can still find 19th-century sofas and wallpaper styles. Let's make the house look splendid again—but as it was when it was ours, at the turn of the present century!"

Amid this clamor, we have overlooked one ghost, a solitary sort who has not had a chance to speak, although he, or she, has been trying all the time. He, or she, is not, you see, a Drayton, at least not so far as we know. This person is the amateur or professional architect who drew up the plans for old John Drayton's mansion in the first place, and then disappeared anonymously from history. The architect desperately wants to add this to the argument:

"No, none of that, please, you Draytons—no restoration to any era. Although I stay among your shades as a humble unknown, my claim for the house is the best. In this whole continent few other structures of such great architectural interest have survived so long. Where else in America is there a building that exhibits so much architectural sophistication from such an early time? I agree that intrusions like the balustrades must go. But otherwise the current owners, the National Trust people, are right to leave the house alone. Its service to high society is ended; you Draytons have finished with it. Now visitors can celebrate it as pure architecture, unbound by time, immortal as a masterwork of art.

"To encourage that, the trust should clear the grounds of other distractions, of course, and just footnote the Drayton family story. The trust should emphasize instead that here is a rarity, a grand structure Palladian in inspiration, like Monticello, but uncluttered with the Jeffersonian inventions that distract the visitor there. Here visitors may study all decorative and structural features unobscured by furnishings; and those features truly are wonderful. By keeping this mansion as it is, the National Trust is returning it to its most original state, as a conception in my head. That is when it was most singular of all!"

Perhaps you find it difficult to believe that such nocturnal discourses can be heard among the shadows in the drafty rooms of Drayton Hall. They represent live voices, nonetheless. They echo views that have been argued at meetings of the Drayton Hall Council and elsewhere in our own time by living—in fact, quite lively—preservationists. Even as I write, the Great Drayton Hall Debate seems far from over.

Leaving the old structure unfurnished, with accumulated additions to the building and grounds intact—is that just indecisiveness, a failure of nerve, as some preservationists have charged? Or is it commendable humility of a kind we need more of in caring for historic sites, so that we don't irreversibly impose on them some passing meaning that appeals to us, some contemporary taste? Perhaps great places ought to be restored to what originally they were intended to stand for, to express, to be. But what then of the past voices, the competing claims for attention in historic preservation, the pleas from historical people not to be left out? At this site, they seem compelling in their totality. I think of how Drayton Hall has survived incredible threats already over nearly 250 years—wars, earthquakes, economic disasters, political upheavals, and recently a hurricane. As its history continues, I hope the grand old place will survive us preservationists as well. I hope we can recognize that ours is but one more voice in the chorus of history.

THE ENSHRINEMENT OF HONEST ABE

IF AN ANCIENT GREEK, SAY PERICLES, THE FAMED leader of classical Athens, came to Hodgenville, Kentucky, he would understand immediately what he saw. There on a rise, a hillside actually, he would see a temple, made of the usual marble, with the usual columns and pediments: the works. He would reach it by patiently laboring up the usual long flight of steps, just as at home. At home, in the fifth century B.C., anyway, such temples would house oracles, such as the one at Delphi. Or they would enshrine gods, such as Athena, whose good will one solicited. Her statue filled the sanctuary of the Athenian Parthenon. Our Greek visitor would recognize the Hodgenville temple as probably dedicated to the God Lincoln, judging from the way his name appears all over the area, along with more puzzling inscriptions, such as "National Park Service." Pericles would suppose this Lincoln some local god, because he isn't in the Greek Pantheon. Or Pericles might take him for an oracle, because he is often quoted by American officials when they wish to sound wise. With thoughts like those, our Greek visitor would mount the steps to this temple on the site of the Sinking Spring Farm, where in 1809 Abraham Lincoln was born, to see what he actually might be.

If Pericles did the same thing at the Lincoln Memorial temple at the end of the Mall in Washington, D.C., he would not be surprised when he looked inside. There sits the God Lincoln, larger than life on a high pedestal, just as Athena sat in the Parthenon. This clearly would be a place to say prayers or offer sacrifices, in hope of supernatural assistance in the struggles of life (chiefly with one's armed neighbors). And so Pericles might pray, or leave money or a little meat, and depart without thinking any more about it.

At Hodgenville, however, he would enter the temple in bewilderment. Inside he would find no statue at all, but just another building—in fact, a distinctly inferior one. It is made of rough logs, not smooth marble. It has chinks daubed with mud instead of being pieced perfectly together like the Parthenon. And its smallness would reveal it as more of a hut for peasants than the dwelling place of a deity. Puzzled, Pericles would peer inside to see what sort of immortal this could attract. He would find just a dirt floor and a crude fireplace. Otherwise, the hut is utterly empty, plain and bare. Then Pericles would doubly shake his head, for obviously what is enshrined is the hut itself.

The National Park Service has custody of the Lincoln birthplace site, including the Sinking Spring and a tree called the Boundary Oak. They were there when the Lincolns were, but the Park Service does not attribute authenticity to the cabin. A Park Service pamphlet describes the hut in the temple as merely like the original birthplace, "simple: a dirt floor, a shingled roof, one window, one door, a small fireplace, and a low chimney made of straw and clay and hard wood. The tiny window square might have been covered with greased paper, an animal skin, or an old quilt to keep out summer insects and the cold winter wind." The park service some time ago decided that available evidence argued against this cabin being the original.

The leading historian of historic preservation, Charles B. Hosmer Jr., assures us that the site itself is the right one. Here, just a short drive south of modern Louisville, Tom Lincoln did once have a farm. Here his wife, Nancy Hanks, did give birth to a son named Abraham a couple of years before they moved somewhere else. This was the Abraham Lincoln who did become one of our most highly regarded presidents, and, at least in our time, the most revered.

The cabin in the temple can be traced only to A.W. Dennett, a New Yorker, Hosmer says, who invented the "quick lunch." Dennett got hold of a hut that may once have stood on the Sinking Spring property, then hired an evangelist minister named Bigham to exhibit it to the public for a fee. (Bigham toured it with another cabin alleged to have been the birthplace of Jefferson Davis.) The Lincoln logs, if you will pardon the expression, somehow later wound up in storage on Long Island. There an editor with *Collier's* magazine eventually found them after Dennett's bankruptcy. *Collier's* executives led a campaign to buy the farm site, restore the cabin to it, and preserve it as a national shrine, all of which the federal government was persuaded to do after the private association formed for the purpose couldn't raise enough money to do so. The temple doubtless cost a lot; and we may well ask along with Pericles what we are exalting at such great expense by building a temple over a muddy looking hut.

Historian Hosmer reports that the builders of the shrine thought of it as a tangible lesson that "democracy is ever humble." They intended the temple and surrounding park to provide a garden spot where visitors from all sections of the country could "find the inspiration of national unity." Those who earlier sought profit in exhibiting famous log cabins at fairs spoke in similar terms. Such a cabin was "a shrine to approach for contrast in spectacle; for realization of the nation's development; for reminder of the country's history through tribulation to triumph."

Perhaps the cabin does convey some such message from the past. But if one stands and looks and ponders, that strange feeling persists. How bizarre to build a temple to preserve a hut! One thinks of what scholars mean when they talk of myth creation. One thinks of the familiar American rags-to-riches myth, and its log-cabin-to-the-White-House variation, using the term "myth" in the sense of something in which one believes without requiring evidence. It doesn't specially matter that you and I are not becoming rich and famous or president of the Greatest Land on Earth. We could do it, and we may yet, because people like Lincoln, of humble origins like us, have risen to prominence out of the common earth—at least those with pioneer spirit. In the Land of Opportunity, every new baby potentially emancipates its parents from their place in the ordinary.

Also we may like it that our great president, who came from a humble cabin, stayed humble when he became great, did not declare himself superior, a god, but remained our peer, a regular guy, in touch with us, The People. It may be Lincoln's common clay that the cabin symbolizes at Hodgenville, not his divinity.

Yet I think all that is highly hypothetical speculation. I think the message of that temple—which its physical character will convey whatever the park service literature may say—is at once more simple and more profound. That cabin is a bit like a piece of the True Cross, a relic that gives tangible reality to a great mystery. After all, how did the child of an obscure Kentucky dirt-farmer become as impressive a leader as our nation has ever known? A trip to Hodgenville and a quiet quarter-hour's communion at the Sinking Spring shrine can leave one as impressed as were the ancient Greeks with the unpredictability of destiny. Honest Abe himself might linger to ponder that. Seeing what we've made of his hut, he would probably also smile.

OLD WORLD WONDERS

ALWAYS IT HAS SEEMED A STRUGGLE FOR ME TO learn what I am supposed to at historic sites. Old World Wisconsin, for example, has so much of significance to teach about ethnic architecture, decorative arts traditions, farming as practiced before self-propelled machines, and the folklife of immigrant Americans. What I remember best from there, however, are a pig, a potato, and fog.

Fog: Is it just to me that the feeling of contact with history is hard to engender under a bright sun? Or do others also feel closer to the past when a thunderstorm breaks over a Civil War battlefield, when a sunset casts shadows around a frontier fort, when mist enshrouds an old, historic house? It won't do to say that we get this from the movies; they have merely exploited a romantic sense of the past that humans had long before film was invented. I don't know where we got it. Perhaps fog can help conjure the past simply because it helps shut out the present. Certainly on the evening when I first visited Old World Wisconsin—the fog growing thicker the closer we approached—I could hardly help feeling that, through it, we were mystically entering history.

Old World Wisconsin is an outdoor ethnic museum, or living history farm. A collection of farms, rather, because, when completed, Old World Wisconsin is to contain some sixteen farmsteads, each representing a different immigrant group at a different time in Wisconsin history. Already, for example, there are a German area, a Finnish area, a Danish area, a Norwegian area, even a Yankee area. Under development in the Yankee area is the Sanford Farm, intended to show a prosperous Yankee's home, buildings, and agricultural operations in the 1860s. The German area contains the 1860 Schulz farm, the 1875 Shottler farm, and the 1880 Koepsell farm. In the Scandinavian areas are farms with even more exotic names: Fossebrekke (1845) and

42

Kvaale (1865) in the Norwegian area, Rankinen (1897) and Ketola (1915) in the Finnish area, and Pedersen (1890) in the Danish area. Trails a half-mile to a mile long enable a visitor to move from site to site in ten-to-fifteen-minute walks. These intervals in themselves provide a kind of time-change tunnel, through which a visitor can leave the atmosphere of one site before entering another. Eventually, farms of many other European nationalities who found land and new lives in 19th-century Wisconsin will fill the beautiful 576-acre enclosure.

Old World is the work of the State Historical Society of Wisconsin. The society's staff began to create it in 1976, in the Kettle Moraine State Forest near Eagle, Wisconsin, as a Bicentennial undertaking. Painstaking research went into it. Historians found and restored log houses, barns, and other farm buildings representative of the styles of each ethnic group, and furnished them with the old stoves, pots, pans, crockery, tables, chairs, plows, pigsties, harnesses, horses, wagons, and other items that one would have seen in and about them at an earlier time. The society hired and trained "interpreters," who wear the particular clothing style of each ethnic group in each time period, and who seem, as one visits the houses and farms, to be going about daily household chores and farm activities. The farms are indeed real, sown with crops like those planted by immigrant settlers, and full of the noises and smells of poultry and cattle. Today's "Old World" farmers, like the predecessors they portray, plant crops and mend fences and roofs when spring comes. They make vinegar and beer in the summer, dry herbs and can produce for winter, and bring in the harvest in a "thresheree" in early fall. They make soap, organize quilting bees, and prepare geese and hogs for market as the cold months set in. Why? "To show the life-style and heritage of the diverse peoples from many countries and backgrounds who came to create a new life on the midwestern frontier," says the society officially, so that "visitors to Old World Wisconsin will rediscover their past."

That is what I read about it as the tour bus on which I rode made its way carefully there through the thickening fog. But such a description seemed stilted in that atmosphere. We were a group of historical-agency administrators, trying to get there in the winter after a meeting in Madison. The interpreters' activities at the site had ended by the time of our arrival, and it was too cold anyway to walk very far outside. But the bus took us by each area, stopping long enough in the semi-darkness to permit inspection through the window glass. In vain would we strive to identify material details—architecture, furnishings, implements. We just silently watched each low cluster of dark buildings eerily materialize through the gloom. They've done it, I kept thinking—they've really accomplished it here. This is another century; I am in it. Here is real history, silent and cold as it should be, encapsulated by the fog.

A pig: What a different sight Old World was when I returned in the midsummer daylight. History then again became something fascinating to study more than to feel. I studiously noted the differences between barns built by Germans and by Finns. I observed with pleasure the strutting roosters and historic hens. And I listened with admiration to a young housewife, in full costume of the early 19th century, as she described her life. I listened, in fact, more closely than I had intended, thinking at first I would just blithely make the rounds.

She was not happy, this historical personage, sitting there churning butter. (Or was she trying to boil water that sultry afternoon, or to mend old clothes? Somehow I associate all of that with what I saw of her.) She and her family had come from the old country in hope of escaping a life of poverty. But so far here, they had experienced little more than imprisonment in this small, wood hut. When would they ever be able to work themselves out of it? The dreariness of Wisconsin's bitter winters, the struggle to bring crops successfully to harvest through the hot months, the unrelenting chores and continuous work, the worries over weather and animals and health—would the milk and honey ever begin to flow? Did I happen to notice whether the hog had gotten out again?

Something like that I heard—something intended to convey a social historian's sense of an immigrant farm woman's reality. Even the stench was there. On impulse, I went looking for that pig. When I found him, he seemed hardly likely to wander from the premises. He appeared, all pink and nearly hairless, wallowing on his side in a patch of mud. No creature ever looked more arrogantly ugly, more self-righteous in its filthiness. The people in the house hoped to eat him eventually. But in the meantime, he owned them; he could compel their concerned attention by wandering away or simply looking ill. He and the mud owned them, he and the hut, he and all the miserable circumstances that, for me, he suddenly personified. How I wanted to rectify all this—to free that miserable young woman from this dreadful animal! Again, at least momentarily, I had transcended my time. Once more, in still another way, history had arisen around me and pulled me in.

A potato: Leaving the pig, I took another short trek on the trail. It brought me to the Raspberry School, named for the Raspberry Bay on Lake Superior. Norwegian and Swedish families there had sent their children to this school from 1896 to 1914. With other visitors, I took one of the rough seats, just as those children had done, and listened attentively to the teacher, another costumed interpreter, who told us what was taught and what the conditions of schooling were like. The details I have forgotten, but the impressions remain vivid. Learning would not have come easily here; children would have had to strive hard, even for rudiments. As the teacher spoke, I felt myself shiver at the thought of trying to study while seeking warmth from the school's little stove.

In winter, I learned, the parents baked potatoes for the children, which they brought to school in their mittens as hand-warmers, then left on the stove to eat for lunch. How sad, I thought—the poor, cold, hungry kids, struggling to learn something. The alternative way of looking at it hardly occurred to me; I did not exalt their bravery, their fortitude, their dedication, the ability of human beings to surmount adversity. I didn't because at that moment I felt too much like one of them, just sitting there feeling, in my imagination, more cold and hungry than heroic. Again, history had reached out, momentarily, to capture me, had drawn me in through the fog.

I mentioned none of this, of course, to the site's admirably professional administrators, nor to my colleagues in the history business on the bus. They might have smiled at my naivete, raised an eyebrow at my sentimental imagination, or even felt insulted by my lack of studiousness at the site. Exactly, I thought, what the teacher often must have felt, there in that old one-room schoolhouse, exasperated with kids who could hardly concentrate on anything except how much time had yet to pass before they got to eat those hot potatoes. Their history textbooks probably told them about George Washington and his tattered, freezing troops nobly holding on at Valley Forge, or about the boy Abe Lincoln, doggedly trying to read in the dingy candle-lit cabin.

But I suppose that even to them—isn't it strange?—such history would have seemed unreal and remote, lost in a kind of fog and far away. As they studied history, they probably never thought of themselves as being in it. But then, do we?

THE RISE AND FALL OF CAIRO, ILLINOIS

YEARS AGO I SAW SOMEWHERE IN KANSAS A ROAD
sign at the edge of a town proudly identifying it as "the geographical
center of the United States." I assume that several cities have had that
status at one time or another as our nation expanded, and today I have
no idea where the addition of Hawaii and Alaska as states has left the
geographical center. I am confident of this, however: the historical center of the United States is in Cairo, Illinois.

That is, I admit, a less than self-evident assertion. But to persuade
oneself of it requires little more than a casual visit to Cairo, which is the
southernmost city in Illinois. More particularly, one should go to the
park that lies just below Cairo at what historically seems to have been
part of Bird's Point. It is best to go with a picnic basket, for what one
sees there is well worth an afternoon's contemplation. One may look
out from a big, raised concrete platform, which has been erected in the
park to look like the prow of a ship. Or one may pick a path down
through the rocks on the shore at the park's extreme southern edge.
From either vantage point one beholds an extraordinary sight: the
junction, the union, the merger of the mighty Mississippi and Ohio
rivers.

For us history-minded souls, aware of how many explorers and settlers made use of these central rivers, of how far up and down and
across the continent they stretch, of how gigantic they are, this is indeed a stunning sight. Back up the eastern shoreline from this point,
one sees the huge bridge that links Kentucky to Illinois over the Ohio
River. Back up the western shoreline from this point, one sees the towering bridge that links Missouri to Illinois over the Mississippi River.
Just below one's feet at the point, one sees the two rivers join, creating
the great waterway that leads down to New Orleans and the Gulf of

Mexico. Through history, thousands of canoes, rafts, barges, and steamboats have made their way past this point. Even in literature, Huck Finn's raft came by that point one fateful foggy night. How devastated Mark Twain's heroes were to find they had missed Cairo, where they could have crossed the Ohio to freedom for Jim in the North.

On my first trip, as I sat there with my shoes off, pausing to dip my toes in the intermingling waters, the thought struck—yes, this is the country's historical center. Everything off to my left, on the north side of the Ohio, was more or less the Historical North—the land of Yankee traders and Midwestern industrialists, of blue uniforms and automobile plants, of New York and Boston, Philadelphia and Pittsburgh, Cleveland and Detroit. Everything below, on both sides of the merger-swollen Mississippi, was more or less the Historical South—the land of plantations and slaves, of gray uniforms and cotton wharves, of Richmond and Charleston, New Orleans and Memphis, Atlanta and Montgomery. Everything off to my right, more or less, was the Historical West, the land of cowboys and Indians, of buckskin clothes and oil gushers, of St. Louis and Denver, San Francisco and Salt Lake, even Honolulu and Anchorage.

Fed from the springs of the Alleghenies and the snows of the Rockies, with help from northern lakes, the two rivers at their merger point show currents wonderfully visible and strong—a swirling motion as seemingly incontrovertible as that of Time itself. Captivated by the sight, I could hardly fail to ask the obvious historical question: If this large strand of land between the two great arteries, this peninsula so similar to Manhattan Island, is where the entire country came together historically, and where so much traffic up and down the nation's central waterways had to pass, then why wasn't something like New York immediately at my back? Why was this no Battery where I sat; why no twin towers of the World Trade Center hovering overhead, no Wall Street within walking distance? Why, a mile or two back up the road from the little park, was there merely Cairo, population 6,000 or so? What happened historically to deprive that perhaps satisfactory but hardly remarkable city of the skyscrapers, the cultural glitter, the financial and political power that seems, on so theoretically superb a site, its natural right? Instead of something like its famed Egyptian namesake on the similarly impressive Nile Delta, here stands only a small town called "Kayro" by its citizens.

Determined to find the explanation, I gathered up my picnic basket, got in my car, drove out of the park, and entered Cairo's city limits. There I went looking for its historical society. Any place this interesting, I reasoned, certainly would have one. From it, perhaps, I could find out what accounted for the absence of grandeur.

Sure enough, out on a pleasant, tree-lined street called Washington Avenue, I found Magnolia Manor, a historic house museum maintained by the Cairo Historical Association. I found my way to it with the help of a commercial postcard that described the mansion as "built of Cairo brick in 1869," adding that "Ulysses S. Grant made his headquarters here during the Civil War," which seemed puzzling in light of the generally accepted fact that the war ended in 1865. But one cannot blame historical societies for commercial postcards, and I followed the walk to the porch of the grand old dwelling, noting (to quote the Historic American Buildings Survey) its "heavy, ornate, uneasy style of architecture." A hand-written sign invited: "please ring bell and wait for custodian." I rang. I waited. No custodian appeared.

Subsequently I discovered that I had simply come at the wrong time. The historical association opened the house to the public only during certain hours of certain days. But that day, as I repeatedly rang the bell, eager for enlightenment, the silence increasingly carried a message of its own. It was this: No historical society would answer the question I had come to ask. Whatever treasures lay preserved in Magnolia Manor, they were not going to explain why Cairo did not become New York City. Historic house museums and historical societies are not maintained to explain what did not happen.

Historians always have speculated about whether fate of some kind controls human affairs, and I soon had cause to wonder. The question that had come to me in Cairo did not go away as I drove back to my home city, where I discovered to my amazement that my trip had coincided with the reissue, by the Southern Illinois University Press, of what it called a "classic local history"—A History of the City of Cairo, Illinois. The author, John M. Lansden, had originally given it to the world in 1910, through the Chicago publishing company of R.R. Donnelley & Sons. Lansden himself died in 1923 after practicing law in Cairo for 57 years; his career included service as city attorney and mayor. Although he was not a trained historian, Lansden combined intimate personal knowledge of much of the town's history with an exceptional willingness to tell the straight truth about controversial issues. Surely here I could find help with my quest to learn why a great city had not arisen on Cairo's site.

Alas, what the book first taught me was my question's lack of originality. As early as 1721, Father Xavier de Charlevoix declared upon reaching the mouth of the Ohio River: "There is no place in Louisiana [by which he meant the great territory drained by the Mississippi] more fit, in my opinion, for a settlement than this, nor where it is of more consequence to have one." On roughly the same spot in 1836, a traveler named Caleb B. Crumb wrote in his diary: "I seem to see in the place of the two houses which at present constitute this un-named village, a noble and flourishing city. . . ." In 1851, Lieutenant Colonel Arthur Cunynghame published in London an account of his visit to the site: "Geographically speaking, there is perhaps no position in the whole of the United States which would promise better for the site of a large city than that of Cairo." In 1859, Jules Rouby published in Paris a *Guide Americain* touting the prospects of the "insignificant village" of Cairo "to become some day an eminent city, a colossal center of progress and of business," because of a geographical "situation almost unrivaled in the entire world. . . ." And so on, with other visitors through the years. As Lansden ruefully remarks, "They all seemed to think that at the junction of two such great rivers as the Ohio and the Mississippi there ought to be a fine, not to say a grand city."

Apparently the first persons actually to act on the notion were French explorers who built a fort and tannery in 1702 somewhere near what is now Cairo. Indians drove them out in what one might consider the city's first rise and fall. At least one subsequent visitor of importance decided against locating there. In 1779, General George Rogers Clark reported to Thomas Jefferson:

> I am happy to find that your sentiments respecting a Fortification at or near the mouth of the Ohio is so agreeable to the Ideas of every man of any judgment in this Department. It is the spot that ought to be strong and Fortified, and all the Garrisons in the Western Country Dependent on it, if the ground would admit it, but the misfortune is, there's not an acre of ground nearer the Point than four miles rise the Ohio, but what is often Ten feet under water.

Rogers built the fort on higher ground downriver. Nonetheless, after Americans drove out the English, the French, and hostile Indians, and organized the Illinois Territory, one John G. Comegys of Maryland and several associates revived the dream. They persuaded the legislature to incorporate the city (and bank) of Cairo. Yet hardly anything followed. Apparently the proprietors lacked adequate capital or energy or both. Lansden identifies other problems. Major Stephen Long, on his expedition to the Rockies in 1819, noted how hard it was to find ground near Cairo high and dry enough to see the giant streams converging. (Reading that, I understood the need for the platform in the park.) Few settlers proved willing to put up with the peninsula's dense forest, its undergrowth of nettles, its swarms of mosquitoes, and the necessity to live in shacks on stilts to escape floods. As late as 1836, even though the steamboat era had begun and traffic burgeoned on the rivers, Cairo remained, in Lansden's words, "a mere woodyard" for steamboat fuel. "The difficulty," he posited, "was obvious enough; a great central position, great rivers coming together, draining an empire in extent, but almost annually claiming dominion over the intervening land they themselves had created."

The Comegys venture collapsed after his death in 1819; his associates forfeited their Cairo lands through failure to make full payment for them. Thus concluded a second unspectacular rise and fall.

A third began in the late 1830s when a new investment group, led by Darius B. Holbrook, took up the still-not-hopeless dream. The chartering that year of the Illinois Central Rail Road Company, which planned to start a rail line near the great rivers' confluence, resurrected developers' hopes. Almost at once temporary cottages went up alongside machine shops, saw mills, foundries, brickyards, drydocks, and other commercial facilities. By 1841, Cairo had even built a steamboat, *The Tennessee Valley*. But river business at Cairo didn't rise fast enough to sustain such operations, and on top of that came bad publicity. In 1842, Charles Dickens traveled through. Lansden decided that Dickens must have been in a fit of pique about other matters when he arrived; but whatever the cause, the great English novelist excoriated Cairo in his *American Notes*:

> We came again in sight of the detestable morass called Cairo; and stopping there took in wood, lay alongside a barge, whose starting timbers scarcely held together. It was moored to the bank, and on

its side was painted "Coffee House"; that being, I suppose, the floating paradise to which the people fly for shelter when they lose their houses for a month or two beneath the hideous waters of the Mississippi.

Lansden admits that "Cairo had a hard name before Dickens saw it. It had a hard name because it was a hard place." Not only did the flooding make life difficult there; the river traffic brought what Lansden called "hard characters."

By 1840, Cairo managed to attract 2,000 inhabitants. But by the mid-forties, says Lansden, "the town had fully entered upon its decline" again. Confronted with the wrath of creditors and citizens alike, Holbrook worked out a deal in 1846 for eastern trustees to take over the property and the enterprise. Cairo's population fell to 242.

In the 1850s, the railroads finally did arrive. Tracks of the Illinois Central and a half-dozen other companies eventually traversed the city, and the population once more grew, from 2,188 in 1860 to 12,566 in 1900. Some obstacles to navigation were removed from the rivers; more important, both of them were bridged. Rail commerce, not riverboats, would give the struggling city such security as it had.

Water continued to threaten that security. Land companies erected small levees, which protected Cairo to some degree. But in the middle 1800s floods broke through periodically, and neither the trustees nor the railroads seemed willing or able to finance adequate protection. Lansden indicates that the trustees shortsightedly discouraged growth by imposing charges for commercial use of Cairo's wharves and by offering lots only for long-term lease, not for sale. Unwilling to invest further in better flood protection, the trustees finally gave the existing levees to the city, with the requirement that it also take over responsibility for maintaining and strengthening them—a burdensome gift that nevertheless seemed the only real hope for Cairo's soggy citizens.

Floods were not the only water problem. The great rivers that ran around Cairo also ran under it, below the sand on which the city rested. Lansden painted the grim picture: "In times of very high waters in the rivers, the city is much like an empty basin sunken almost to its brim. The minutest opening in the bottom of the vessel will permit a stream of water to shoot up almost to the level of the brim." At low water the seepage receded, which happily kept Cairo dry enough to avoid malaria and other diseases related to swamps; but when the rivers ran high, flooding from seepage was something no levee could prevent. Although Lansden argued for earth-filling as the solution, the city was unable to afford it except under the streets. In the 1870s, the city's effort to finance street-fills by property assessments ran into legal problems, and when the city stopped interest payments on its bonds, it had to deal with more litigation, none of which encouraged municipal growth.

The sad catalogue of Cairo's 19th-century problems included a lack of good ferry facilities across the great rivers before they were bridged. Their breadth and unstable shorelines made them barriers rather than sources of prosperity. Political bickering hurt as well. "In these more modern times," Lansden recounts, "we often hear it enjoined upon the business and leading men in the community to get together; but in Cairo for three or four decades such an expression was never heard." From 1857 to 1909 the city had seventeen mayors, and in the early 20th century its reputation grew as a wide open town. An increase in saloon fees in 1909 added substantially to the annual revenues of the municipality. In that same year, Cairo attracted undesirable notoriety from lynchings there of a black man charged with rape and a white man charged with murder. The only extended notice of Cairo in Donald Tingley's scholarly study of the history of Illinois from 1899 to 1928 deals with that event.

The Cairo story is not wholly negative. Lansden chronicles the creation of schools and churches and civic organizations, the construction of some fine residences and public buildings, and the near-heroic efforts of several individuals to cope with the city's problems. Over the long term, Cairo did not exactly fall; it just never really rose, not in a grand manner anyway—except at one point that I have left out of the account above. When the Civil War broke out, the Union made Cairo a platform for attack.

Within ten days of the firing on Fort Sumter, troops from Chicago rushed downstate to secure Cairo against a Southern threat to take it. From there, the North could control traffic on both the Ohio and the Mississippi rivers and block the flow of contraband south from St. Louis. Fort Defiance went up on the riverbank as thousands of solders came through, eventually including Confederate captives from the campaigns to the south. General Grant set up headquarters in Cairo (though not in Magnolia Manor) in 1861. From there and from related river ports the Union launched gunboat and troop movements that ultimately gave it control of Tennessee and of the Mississippi River south, splitting the Confederacy.

Mud ran in Cairo's streets, but money ran into the pockets of its merchants. Buildings rose, rents rose faster, and prices of goods rose faster yet. Writes Lansden: "Cairo having become a great military station and depot, money soon began to make its appearance in a way never dreamed of by any one in the town, nor, for that matter, by any of the somewhat visionary founders of the place."

Prominent among the merchant suppliers of federal troops was flour miller Charles A. Galigher, who built Magnolia Manor after the war and furnished it lavishly. He entertained General Grant there in 1880, after the latter had been president; and that seems to have been the high point of Cairo's entire history. Today the city's historical association preserves the grand mansion, the fine furnishings, the Civil War mementos, and the bed in which Grant slept—the surviving evidence, in short, of Cairo's historical high-water mark. What the museum preserves is the highest point to which the city rose.

I returned once to Cairo. This time I brought with me my edition of the 1949 *American Guide* volume on the Lakes States, which describes Cairo's historic Ohio Street. "Once noisy with traders, steamboatmen, and travelers of all kinds," says the *Guide*, it is "now lined with deserted taverns, warehouses, and stores." As I drove the street looking even for those, I felt again that eerie sense of silence that had come to me earlier at the old house. Much of once-bustling Ohio Street today consists of weed-covered, gaping, vacant lots.

Oh well, I thought, finding my way once more to the park, to the point where the still-impressive rivers merge. However evident the limits of its history, who can say that Cairo will not someday rise again? However explainable, it still seems wrong for there not to be something grander at this remarkable site—something more wonderful at our great nation's historical center.

Or is there a message in that, too? Which is actually more central, more typical in the urban experience of Americans—the onward and upward progress we associate with New York or Chicago? Or the rises and falls of a Cairo, Illinois?

ARE WE SEEING ANY HISTORY YET?

SOMETIMES HISTORY SEEMS MOST ELUSIVE IN THE hands of those who know it best. Take for example the views expressed in a significant book about historic sites that the Smithsonian Institution Press published, *Past Meets Present: Essays About Historic Interpretation and Public Audiences,* edited by Jo Blatti. In it, eleven professionals who work with museums, historic sites, or "material culture" elsewhere relate their different notions of what history is.

The Betsy Ross House in Philadelphia is historic, right? Not especially, says Pierce Lewis, a cultural geographer. It is no more historic than the homes of factory workers in Woonsocket, Rhode Island, and it is a less "truthful" museum than modern-day South Philadelphia. Why? Because it is marked off, frozen, out of context. History is not a place; it is a "dimension." To Lewis, it makes no more sense to rope off a house as historic, implying that what's inside the rope has more history than what's outside it, than it does to say there is more geography in one place than in another. If you know how to read the patterns that history weaves in places, the entire world can be studied as a museum.

All right, then, how about Brooklyn Heights? That entire area is designated a historic preservation landmark district. Better, right? No, writes Elizabeth Collins Cromley, an architectural historian. Brooklyn Heights preserves only a cleaned-up, pleasant sense of history. It is "a historically atmosphered space where genteel values are promoted through tasteful architecture." Yuppies have replaced 19th-century workingmen and turned their old boarding houses into expensively charming residences. There is more "truthful" history in the nearby Two Bridges area, Cromley says. It is not designated a historic district, but there elements of the past persist without a cut-off in the continuation of urban change.

For honesty, then, how about Plimoth Plantation? Among historic sites, it is famous for its realism. It presents Pilgrim life complete with all the filth, hard labor, lack of privacy, and other dreary conditions of existence in the wilderness. Nope, writes Michael Ettema, a curator at the Henry Ford Museum and Greenfield Village. Plimoth Plantation gives a lot of information about life in 1628, but why do we need it? Nothing there is related to the present. Plimoth exhibits material conditions but doesn't explain material change or show its effects on social structures and human relationships. For example, we learn what Pilgrims wore, but not how they used clothing to assert status, express personality, or reinforce sex roles, as compared with the functions of dress in other times. In fact, by showing how unpleasant things were in the past, Plimoth only underscores an ideological notion, "that modern technology results in a superior existence and that it is the only logical course for humanity, that the only real choice in life is to sustain progress, and that is best done materially."

What about a site significant not for how people lived but for what they achieved? How about Valley Forge? No, material realism is not enough there either, says Irene Burnham. She helped plan a museum for the Valley Forge Historical Society. It has a "reality room" all right—exhibits about what actually happened—but also a "symbolism area." The latter shows how the success of Washington's tattered troops in surviving the winter in retreat has become a powerful symbol of triumph over adversity, a symbol "that still lives" and "prevails in our patriotic vocabulary. . .an evolved symbol with its own history."

Then how about the things with which we waged important wars? How about the old aircraft carrier *Intrepid*, which was outfitted in the Hudson River as the Sea-Air-Space Museum? There is hardly a sign of history there, writes Michael Wallace, a professor of "radical" history. The *Intrepid* exhibits lots of past and present weapons, but barely acknowledges their relationship to war, let alone to the horrors of it.

Nor is the development of Ellis Island as a historic site likely to have much real history either, Wallace fears, if celebrants of the American melting pot myth develop the site uncritically.

Ellis Island is the famed transfer point for millions of immigrants into America. Dwight Pitcaithley of the National Park Service and historian Michael Frisch see it in still another way. They complain that the other writers pay no attention to visitors at historic sites, except as persons who ought to be correctly instructed there. But we visitors come to places such as Ellis Island with varied and sometimes vivid notions of our own. Site interpreters must start with what we already think is history and what we want to learn.

Warren Leon of Old Sturbridge Village seems to agree, but thinks visitors ought to be shaken up, challenged, disoriented, and given exhibits in which we have to figure out the history. Jo Blatti, a consultant, thinks historians can't in any case "recreate the past in any literal way," but can hope only to discern, in a phrase attributed to George Kubler, "the shape of time."

As if history had not become nebulous enough in all that, Jane Greengold, an artist, explains how she invented stories and works of art to explain the history of a big pond on Manhattan Island. Once it was an important source of water. Today its site is but a dip in the streets east of Broadway. To grasp the full reality of historical change requires fiction, she says; the thing itself has disappeared from sight. Indeed. Here once again, as so often in this book, I wanted to cry out: "Aren't we seeing any history yet?!"

Such is the frustration of a nonetheless fascinating set of arguments. Underneath them all, when taken more seriously, is a discernible consensus. In separate ways, the authors more or less concur that history is not places, things, events, dates, personalities. It is processes, patterns, relationships, changes, continuities, and influences bearing on the present. At its heart, theirs is the familiar academic argument against using the past to prop up present values, ideas, institutions, social status, and behavioral expectations, instead of analyzing critically the continuing effects of past decisions and developments. That is hard to argue against.

But it is also hard to make tangible things convey intangible ideas. I am not sure that history museums should try to compete with books as a medium for abstract analysis. There is truth of a kind in the things we can see and touch and feel. Historic sites may need to concentrate on showing that historical experience was not abstract.

HUNTING FOR HISTORY

EVERY YEAR THOUSANDS OF AMERICANS LOAD UP in cars and RVs to search for history. We head for battlefields, famous trails, homes of past presidents—any site that might still yield the feeling of things past. We seek the sensation of seeing the actual spot where Washington slept, where Custer fell, where the wagons struggled west. On such a quest my brother and I sat in his car way out in one of the emptiest parts of Wyoming. He studied the squiggly lines on his topographical map. He shook his head and said: "I just don't recognize where we are."

We had supposed ourselves to be on the old Bozeman Trail, or Bozeman Cutoff, Bozeman Road, Montana Road, Virginia City Road—those who used it more than a hundred years ago gave it various names. The gold rush to Montana after the Civil War had brought it into being. John Bozeman first traced it in 1864 from Fort Laramie, down on the Oregon Trail, almost straight northwest to the Virginia City gold field, right through the heart of the Sioux Indians' last abundant hunting ground. In 1865 and 1866, U.S. commissioners tried to buy peaceable access to it in treaties with the Cheyennes and Arapahos as well as the Sioux. In the summer of 1866, the government dispatched Colonel H.B. Carrington with units of the 18th U.S. Infantry to go up the trail to establish three forts to protect travelers on it. That expedition culminated disastrously in Red Cloud's War, the Fetterman Massacre, and abandonment of the trail in 1868.

The journal Carrington's wife published about these events had long fascinated my brother and me. By car, we wanted not only to follow the trail where we could, but also to find where Carrington's expedition had camped each day on the way up to the fort sites. Our history hunt, however, had begun to prove difficult. My brother reiterated, "If the map's right, I'm lost, and that makes me mad. I've been reading topo-graphical maps out here for years."

My brother, Gene George, is an independent petroleum geologist based in Casper, Wyoming. We were parked in terrain he had studied, in cattle country owned by ranchers he had met, near sites where he had drilled for oil. By comparing Mrs. Carrington's descriptions of camp sites with features on his topographical maps, he had identified the historic places. One camp had been at the head of Sage Creek. To get to it, we had turned off the hard-surface road that today runs over part of the old Bozeman Trail, then bumped along a rutted dirt road until we reached an abandoned ranch house.

"This is where it should be," he said. "But I'm not seeing here the Sage Creek that I'm seeing on the map."

In Wyoming, of course, a "creek" can be dry most of the year. Its bed can appear as little more than a ravine, a depression in the rolling, sage-covered landscape that stretches openly, unobstructed by trees, for miles and miles.

"This has to be it," I declared blithely. "Probably the creek bed has just filled in some from a century ago. See—there's kind of a dip run-ning along here. At the fork back there, we took what the map shows to be the Ross Road, the old Bozeman Trail. Now we've come the right distance to reach Sage Creek, just off to the left, as your map shows." I gave way in my imagination to the sight of wagons, oxen, mules, horses, and blue-suited soldiers settling in for the night right here, where now we saw around us, apart from one windmill and a dilapidated ranch building, only open grazing land and blue sky.

"Yeah, maybe so," Gene said. "Well, let's go look for the next camp site."

Next we sought the South Fork of the Cheyenne River, fifteen miles farther up the trail, not a bad day's plodding by wagon train. The mo-ment our modern road dropped down over a ridge I recognized the scene. There lay a beautiful camp site—a Wyoming stream with water actually in it, cottonwood trees rustling along beside it, and a lovely grass meadow sheltered by a ridge. Not only did this look like a perfect camp site, combining abundant water, wood, and grassy forage needed by travelers in the old days; it was a camp site still. There in the little meadow stood the bright-colored tents and pick-up trucks of visiting hunters.

"See, we're in the right place!" I exclaimed. "This obviously is it, the camp site on the Cheyenne!" Again, the present scene gave way in my mind to a circle of wagons in the meadow, soldiers leading animals down to the stream and gathering firewood, Mrs. Carrington relaxing under a cottonwood, making the daily entry in her diary:

> South Fork of the Cheyenne, where there is plenty of grass and timber; but the great body of the water, in extremely dry weather, passes under the sand and needs slight digging to start it to the surface and secure an abundant supply. . . .

Well, so what if water appeared more abundant here now? We were here in early fall, not in the dry mid-summer when the Carrington expedition camped. Then I recalled that at the Sage Creek site we had found less water than she had described; to be exact, none. Why more water than she recorded in one place and less in another? But the distance was right, and the river was the right one. If the Carringtons hadn't camped here, they certainly should have.

"Maybe so," my brother allowed. But he went on puzzling over his map, shaking his head.

Suddenly, one of the hunters' trucks came toward us. My brother got out of our car and motioned for the hunters to stop. They did. They listened. They peered at his map. They peered down toward the river. They pointed. Then they talked and pointed and talked some more. Gene came back to the car with a disgusted grin on his face.

"We are not on the Ross Road," he said, "so we are not on the Bozeman Trail. The Ross Road forks off above where we turned; we missed it. Back there we were not at Sage Creek, and this is not the camp site on the Cheyenne River."

The soldiers, the wagons, the animals, Mrs. Carrington—all vanished instantly from my mind's eye. Lost also was that delicious feeling of being in touch with history, of seeing what "they" saw, of experiencing what their time was like. Instead I suddenly felt angry, as if history had abused my trust. I felt undeservedly cheated; I felt a fool.

We backtracked many miles, found the right Ross Road turn-off, followed it along the real Bozeman Trail. Sure enough, Sage Creek unmistakably appeared where my brother's map showed it, to his great satisfaction. Fifteen miles farther brought us to the real camp site on the Cheyenne, less lush than the one we earlier mistook for it, but more in conformance with Mrs. Carrington's description. By then, however, something of the thrill of discovery had gone. The initial disappointment had led me to realize that all we could be sure of anyway was proximity. The Bozeman Trail was not a clearly defined hard-top road or even a set of wagon tracks that everybody had followed. Some had veered here, some there; some may have strayed far from the initial trail in search of grass not already overgrazed by passing animals. Mrs. Carrington herself had written, on the day after the stop here on the Cheyenne, something about "avoiding Humphrey's old camp."

The same thought had occurred earlier when we found the approximate site of Bridger's Ferry, where the expedition also had camped. How much had the North Platte River's course changed in the intervening century, and where, exactly, had the Carringtons crossed? Mrs. Carrington had marveled in her journal about the grand entrance to "Phisterer Canyon," where we found the North Platte now too high to admit wagon passage. Where had they actually entered it?

At old Fort Laramie, where my brother and I had started this trip, we also had looked for history without quite finding it. The National Park Service maintains the fort now as a national historic site. Some buildings survive intact, but others remain only in walls or foundations. Today the fort seems a frustrating miscellany of ruins mixed with restored structures painted to look new.

Should the park service have restored Fort Laramie to its original appearance? Which original appearance? That of the first fort on the site, Fort William, in 1834? Or the one that replaced it, Fort John, in 1841? Or the Fort Laramie that the Army built after buying the site in 1849? Or the expanded Fort Laramie through which the Carrington Expedition passed in 1866? Or the much-altered fort as it existed when finally abandoned by the Army in 1890? Fort Laramie seldom looked the same in any of the intervening years.

However, before day's end, we felt some relief from our frustration. Not far from Fort Laramie, we finally did pin down some history that had stayed put. Just south of the Platte River, a short drive west of the fort, is Register Cliff, where immigrants on the Oregon and Bozeman Trails carved their autographs. Farther upriver are some ruts in the rocks that testify to the passage of thousands of their wagons. The configuration of the terrain is such that nearly every trail traveler, including the Carringtons, apparently had to pass precisely at that place. No map consulting, no guessing, no supposing—the ruts are as clear as can be. History happened here! Once again, the image came to mind of oxen struggling up the rise, dragging covered wagons through these ruts in the rock, bearded men in battered hats goading the straining animals on, women like Mrs. Carrington enduring the jolts inside.

"This I like," Gene said, standing by the ruts. I acknowledged that I felt better, too.

Heading cheerfully home at day's end, we took comfort in noting that we also had seen the same landforms that had been so striking to travelers on the Bozeman Trail. Mrs. Carrington had noted them all—Laramie Peak, which eventually disappeared as the expedition went up the trail; the Bighorn Mountains, which suddenly came to view, dramatic in the distance; the Pumpkin Buttes, almost the only high points off on the other side. Those great landmarks surely had not changed much from the way she saw them.

"No, erosion is very slow," my geologist brother observed. But landforms, alas, are not eternal either. Much of Wyoming once lay under water, long ago in geological time. Strange creatures may have been swimming then where we were driving now. Interior pressures had thrust the mountains up; wind and water had been wearing them down again. "Nature is always trying to level it all out," Gene explained. A sobering thought. If nature succeeds, mere history will of course be submerged irretrievably.

Somehow, however, the knowledge that things are constantly changing does not diminish the human need to experience them as they once were. In response to demands from its visitors, the Park Service will go on maintaining markers at the "exact spot" where Custer and each of his soldiers fell in the Battle of the Little Bighorn. My brother and I will continue compulsively trying to pinpoint Carrington camp sites on the Bozeman Trail. And the wagon ruts in the century-old road will remain far more exciting to tourists today than they ever were to those who had to pass over them. All will continue to stir our imaginations, the more so because nature slowly wears the evidence of human passage away.

Were we looking for historical campsites that day? Or for faith in the durability of things human, for hedges against time? A little of that, perhaps. But more likely for vicarious excitement. Indian wars, frontier troops, pioneers in wagon trains. The ruts brought us closer to them.

Relics of the past provide a base on which the imagination can build, a point of contact with what we suppose to have been the real thing. What else are "historic sites" but a medium, as it were, through which to try to reach the historical spirit world? Sometimes we can almost do it.

AN OPEN LETTER TO
THE BOZEMAN TRAIL ASSOCIATION

Fort Phil Kearny/Bozeman Trail Association
Sheridan, Wyoming

Dear Colleagues:

As a member in good standing, I beg your consideration of my views—my fears—about what could happen at the site of old Fort Phil Kearny on the Bozeman Trail.

On my most recent trip, I saw the beginnings of development of that historic site. I saw where flags have been put up to mark the corners of the long-gone fort's boundaries. I saw the poles with the peepholes in them to point visitors to Pilot Hill, Lodge Trail Ridge, and other significant spots in the surrounding landscape. I toured the newly erected visitors' center, inspected the admirable exhibit work inside, and viewed the introductory video show about the extraordinary events of 1866 to 1868. What worries me is that I understand someone has now proposed to reconstruct the fort itself.

Contemplating that on my recent visit, I understood as never before how the Sioux must have felt, spying from the surrounding hills in 1866, as they watched Colonel Carrington's U.S. troops construct the original fort—the intrusion that provoked Red Cloud's War and led to the Fetterman Massacre nearby. Like the Sioux more than a century ago, I found myself, now, wanting to stop any new construction there. For it seems to me that in such attempts to expand public attention to the site's story, we are in danger of forgetting the essence of it, how it ended, what it meant. The significance of the whole bloody and disastrous episode lies not in the fort's erection but in its burning down.

From the journal Margaret Carrington kept on the original expedition to establish the fort, from the official government investigation afterwards, from Dee Brown's modern history of the Fetterman Massacre, and from the work of other historians, we have the story in considerable detail—the story of a battle of greater strategic importance than the subsequent and more celebrated occurrence on the bluffs above the Little Bighorn. More men died with Custer than died with Fetterman, but at the Little Bighorn, Indians overwhelmed only Custer's contingent. That same day they failed to inflict a similar disaster on the entrenched forces of Major Reno and Captain Benteen less than just five miles away. They retreated and scattered when reinforcements appeared, and from then on for months they found themselves on the run until finally subdued or defeated. After the Fetterman Massacre, in clear contrast. . . but let me recount in proper order the significant points of the Fort Phil Kearny story.

Red Cloud

Red Cloud knew that the land through which the Bozeman Trail cut was the last great hunting ground the Sioux could hope to occupy.

This was the land between the Black Hills on the east and the Bighorn Mountains to the west, north of the Platte River and south of the Yellowstone River. Here the Oglalas and other bands of Teton Sioux had pushed aside the Crows and warred upon the Pawnees, Shoshonis, and Utes to occupy and hold a teeming hunting ground. Here prairie grasses rich in nutrients supported enormous herds of buffalo. Here also in abundance roamed elk, antelope, and deer to be hunted, along with smaller game, including rabbits and sage hens. Here were trout to be taken from the many streams that flowed out of the Bighorns, streams that watered the stands of cottonwood that dotted the basins of rivers named the Powder, the Bighorn, the Tongue. Here grew wild fruits and berries to be gathered, and ample forage for horses. And here lay sheltered areas, where the cold winters could be passed in relative ease and comfort. Here was still the good life as the Sioux knew it.

Red Cloud also knew the dangers of white encroachment on this land. He had heard around the winter fires in his youth such recollections as the old people had of how the advance of the white men had devastated tribes along the Missouri River, how the Sioux had spread down into the plains under pressure from enemy Crees armed with white men's guns, how the whites themselves had soon appeared along the waterways. He himself had watched in wonder as wagon after wagon came lumbering along the Platte, eventually to disappear over South Pass towards California, Utah, or the Oregon Country, until it seemed that the white men's territory had to be drained of population. He had shared the anxiety of his tribe when the stream of travelers instead proved endless, when they destroyed or drove game away from the river bottoms, and when their diseases brought death to the Indians who traded with, begged from, or otherwise made contact with them. Long before Red Cloud's time, epidemics of white men's smallpox had broken the strength of the Arikaras, clearing the way for the Sioux themselves to follow the buffalo out over the plains.

But Red Cloud also knew of more recent aggravations. He knew of the pieces of paper that white men always and forever were wanting the Sioux to put marks on down at Fort Laramie, on the Platte River where the soldiers stayed. Sioux leaders who did that could be designated chiefs of their people by the whites. They could get coffee, tobacco, brown sugar, army blankets, bright-colored cloth, flour, bacon, steers to butcher, and even knives, powder, and guns. Then the soldiers would expect the Sioux to cease molesting whites on the trail, no matter how many came or what they did. Even the Crows were then to be exempt from Sioux warriors' annual summer raids. Such a "treaty" had been "signed" at Horse Creek near Fort Laramie when Red Cloud was a young man. He had seen afterward what the soldiers could do, how a white lieutenant's men killed Conquering Bear after his Brulé band ate a strayed Mormon cow. The Brulés killed all 29 men in the lieutenant's troop in retaliation, but General Harney subsequently found and destroyed Little Thunder's band of Brulés, killing 136 and dragging the rest in chains back to Fort Laramie.

Red Cloud's own Oglalas then had split, the Bear People seeking safer hunting grounds south of the Platte, the Smoke People (Red Cloud among them) fleeing north to the Powder River country. Some Sioux bands still hung around the fort—the "Laramie loafers," who resigned themselves to dependence on white hand-outs and protection. More hot-headed Sioux continued to raid the growing white traffic over the Platte River trail. But the soldiers, Red Cloud knew, could not be depended on to discriminate between hostile and peaceful tribes. Word of how Colonel Chivington's troops massacred friendly Cheyennes at Sand Creek eventually stirred fear and fury in Sioux, Arapahoes, and Cheyennes all up and down the northern plains. Thereafter, when again the whites sought peace, offering presents in exchange for marks on paper, Red Cloud—himself a celebrated war party leader by then—was conspicuous among those who did not "come down."

No, not until the whites and their wagons started leaving the Platte to cut a swath northwest through the grass and game of the Powder River country. Gold, discovered in Montana, lured them over what came to be called the Bozeman Trail. In 1864 and 1865, the traffic grew, threatening the game, despite Sioux harassment. The unusually bitter winter of 1865-1866 made things worse. Only then did Red Cloud listen to the white men's appeals for new treaty negotiations. Appearing at Fort Laramie at last, he rose at the "peace conference" to orate against the whites' invasion of the last land in which the Sioux could feed themselves. Even as he spoke, eight companies of the 2nd Battalion of the 18th U.S. Infantry under Colonel Henry B. Carrington, dusty from a long march up the Platte, rested in camp some four miles east of the fort. What Red Cloud did not know, before coming to consider peace, was that Carrington had orders to march up the Bozeman Trail, to secure it for white passage, to take possession of it, no matter who signed what.

Carrington

What Colonel Carrington knew was how to build a fort.

Not that he was trained for it; he had little training for anything military. He had wanted to be a soldier, but ill health kept him out of West Point. He went to Yale instead, where he took a law degree, then entered into practice in Ohio.

Near the outbreak of the Civil War, Ohio's governor—Carrington's former law partner—appointed him adjutant general. As Fort Sumter fell, Carrington organized the 18th Regiment, of which he then was appointed commanding colonel. But he never led it into battle. The politicians valued his abilities as recruiter and organizer. They kept him employed on the home front, in Indiana as well as in Ohio, while his regiment distinguished itself in the field and took heavy losses. Maybe he wanted to get into the action, maybe he ducked opportunities for it; the evidence is not clear. Once the war ended, however, his political connections put him back at the regiment's head, marching toward hostile Indian country as commander of the Mountain District of the U.S. Army's Department of the Platte.

Even at the outset, he had only about 700 men to protect civilian travel over some 400 miles of trail by building and garrisoning three forts in the heart of Sioux territory. What he and his officers knew of the Mountain District came largely from old copies of the reports of Lewis and Clark. They studied fort building in treatises by a West Point engineering professor, but that art they learned wonderfully well. Indeed, the eight-foot stockade they raised as the middle fort of the three won praise from an informed visitor as the second-best fort in North America, matched only by one owned by the Hudson's Bay Company.

Building it was not easy. First came the long march itself, 236 miles up the Bozeman Trail from Fort Laramie to what Carrington decided was the right site for the middle fort—a sizable plateau between Big Piney and Little Piney creeks, just above their confluence, at the edge of the beautiful Bighorn Mountains. Meadows of thick grass in the vicinity offered rich forage for horses and other stock. Not far off, stands of towering, straight pine trees would provide the hundreds of logs required for a stockade of the size and strength that Carrington envisioned. This fort would need to be stronger than the loose aggregations of buildings that the Army called forts at such places as Laramie, where there were more whites and traffic.

The day after Carrington had appeared with his troops at Fort Laramie, he had attended the "peace" conference there. He had failed at that meeting to assure the Indian "chiefs" of his intent only to maintain peace, and he may narrowly have escaped a knife in the back. Red Cloud and his followers, furious at the arrival of fresh troops in the middle of the peace talks, had vanished from the conference and soon renewed their harassment of whites, including Carrington's troops when they did start up the Bozeman Trail. Woe to the soldier who got separated from his comrades, and goodbye to stock that strayed or grazed under loose security.

Carrington stationed two companies at Fort Reno, the first garrison on the gold mine route, and sent two companies farther up the trail to establish Fort C. F. Smith near the Bighorn River. His remaining four companies and civilian employees went to work on the central fort, named for Civil War hero Philip Kearny. Three-and-a-half months later, after continuous alarms of Indian hit-and-run raids on woodcutters and herds of stock, the fort stood ready for dedication. More than 12,000 logs formed stockade walls, blockhouses, and some twenty other buildings. The walls enclosed a quartermaster's yard and a 400-foot-square stockade, inside which was a large parade ground bordered by a "street" twenty feet wide. On the last day of October 1866, 360 officers and men—some, like Carrington himself, with wives and children along—assembled to watch the Stars and Stripes rise to the top of the 124-foot flagpole. A regimental band, of which Carrington was proud and protective, played "The Star-Spangled Banner," and Carrington himself delivered an oration:

> The steam whistle and the rattle of the mower have followed your steps in this westward march of empire. You have built a central post that will bear comparison with any for security, completeness, and adaptation to the ends in view, wherever the other may be located, or however long in erection. [This] is the first full garrison flag that has floated between the Platte and Montana.

It must indeed have been a magnificent sight, that bright-colored, oversized cloth rectangle, fluttering high above the stockade, a proud sight to those who had devoted themselves to the fort's construction day after day for months. Simultaneously, however, Red Cloud and his allies had devoted themselves daily to attacking travelers on the Bozeman Trail. Many gold-seekers got through by staying in large wagon trains, for the Sioux waged war by hit and run, not by frontal assault, even when they had numerical superiority. But Carrington himself knew that no one moved on the route without danger. What he did not know, as he proudly surveyed his fine fort—what he would learn at frightful cost in less than two months from its dedication—was that he had been building his own prison.

Fetterman

What Captain William J. Fetterman knew was how to fight Confederates.

He had in fact distinguished himself doing it in the regiment Carrington theoretically had headed. At Corinth, Stone's River, Kennesaw Mountain, Peach Tree Creek, Jonesboro, the Siege of Atlanta—all through the Union's campaign from Tennessee down into Georgia, he won commendations for gallantry, bravery, fighting spirit. In 1862 he rose to command the regiment's 2nd Battalion—the unit Carrington would later take into Sioux country to build his splendid fort; and by the Civil War's end, Captain Fetterman had been breveted lieutenant colonel.

A staff assignment took him away from his battalion until late fall of 1866. Then he, too, was ordered up the Bozeman Trail. He arrived at Fort Phil Kearny just three days after the ceremony celebrating its completion. Here he found his old outfit, full of raw recruits but still officially the unit he had seen through some of the most bitter fighting in the Civil War, now sitting contentedly in a pretty stockade. Small wonder that he felt contempt for Carrington. Small wonder that he felt unawed by poorly armed, undisciplined, skirmishing little bands of "uncivilized" Sioux.

Fetterman urged action. He pressed his untested superior to carry the fight out of the fort, to take the offensive. Carrington cited his small troop count to justify caution, pending reinforcements for which he had pled. Defensively, he finally let the insistent Fetterman set a night ambush to catch Indians who had been driving off stock. (No Sioux showed up that night, except on the other side of the fort, where they successfully stampeded another herd of cattle.) But Carrington would not let the disgruntled Fetterman openly take the field against the Indians, to test whether he could whip a thousand of them with a single regular Army company, as he was said to have bragged he could do, or ride safely through the entire Sioux nation with eighty men, another boast attributed to him. Only when the wood train came under attack (yes—Carrington went on building) did he let Fetterman ride out with a relief party. Even then, Carrington insisted that Fetterman simply drive off, not pursue, the harassing Indians. Even then he told Fetterman under no circumstance to chase the attackers over the Lodge Trail Ridge. Not just once, either, but twice (Carrington swore at the inquiry afterwards) he repeated that order before Fetterman got out of the fort at the head of his eighty-man relief party: "Relieve the wood train but do not pursue." Fetterman pursued anyway, nobody knows positively why; on the bright, cold morning of December 21, 1866, Indian decoys drew Fetterman and all eighty of his men over the Lodge Trail Ridge. Fetterman did know how to fight. What he did not know was that Red Cloud was as much a fighter as he, and also as effective a politician, a recruiter, and an organizer as Carrington was. With other leaders, this Red Cloud, who had once killed the war-leader Bull Bear in a civil war among his own Oglala people, had put together, up on the Tongue River not fifty miles from Fort Phil Kearny, a force of 3,000 to 4,000 warriors. Their tipis, reported the Crows, spread over forty miles—not just Oglalas but also Minneconjous and other bands of Sioux, along with Arapahoes and Northern Cheyennes. It was rare for any coalition of Indians to be persuaded to act in concert for more than a day or two. But this was also one of the largest Indian armies any "chief" had yet put together against the United States. Fetterman had no inkling that down along Peno Creek, just beyond the Lodge Trail Ridge, as many as two thousand "unsophisticated savages" had in turn set a trap for him and his eighty men.

The Massacre

Within forty minutes, Fetterman and his troops no longer knew anything. Their bodies lay freezing and hideously mutilated on the slope where a relief party found them.

Carrington did venture out of his fort far enough to recover the dead, once the Indians had seemed to withdraw. But he knew then that without reinforcements, his splendid stockade could be overrun by Red Cloud's army at any time. He doubled the guard night and day despite near-blinding snow. He set up a procedure to blow up the women and children with the powder magazine should the Indians get over the walls. And he sent John "Portugee" Phillips with others out into the blizzard to carry the news down the trail and to get help. In a ride that would immortalize him as the Paul Revere of the West, Phillips made it over the nearly two hundred miles to Horseshoe Station, where he sent the first word by telegraph, then struggled through snow another forty miles to Fort Laramie. There, looking like an apparition from the Ice Age, he burst in on the garrison's Christmas ball. All the while the Indians warmed themselves in their tents, content for the moment with what they knew was, at last, a major victory.

On January 16, 1867, a column of half-frozen soldiers under Lieutenant Colonel Henry W. Wessels arrived to reinforce the terrified garrison of Fort Phil Kearny. Wessels's orders included relieving Carrington of the fort's command. With the women and children, Carrington and his regimental headquarters staff in turn now braved the snow. Temperatures far below freezing made cold slush of hot coffee and compelled the use of axes to cut meat and bread. Among those never to forget this retreat—this exodus—was Frances Grummond. Pregnant, widowed by the massacre, but insistent on taking out with her the pine box that contained her officer-husband's remains, she grimly hung on within a continuously swaying, jolting army wagon, praying to reach Laramie safely. For Carrington, the journey only brought closer a presidentially ordered investigation. Years later, after Carrington's first wife died, Frances Grummond would become his second and spend much of her life helping him try to clear his name.

And Red Cloud? As the weather warmed in late spring, he resumed attacks on the Bozeman Road and the harassment of Fort Phil Kearny. It mattered little that in the summer his warriors failed in two efforts to overwhelm other isolated groups of soldiers, one guarding woodcutters, another in a hayfield. Armed with new repeating rifles, the soldiers at both places took a heavy toll of the surprised Sioux. But a nation whose railroads would, in any case, soon provide satisfactory access to the goldfields by other routes reacted with peace overtures to the shock of the Fetterman disaster. Once again, white emissaries beseeched Red Cloud and his confederates to come down to Fort Laramie. He would consider peace, he responded, when the whites closed down their road and the blue-coats abandoned Forts Reno, C. F. Smith, and Phil Kearny—all three.

In the spring of 1868, the United States gave up. Just six years, more or less, from the first incursion, the government closed the Bozeman Trail. By August, the last troops pulled their wagon trains out of all three forts. Even before the soldiers marched out of sight, according to some accounts, the Indians set fire to Fort Phil Kearny, burning it to the ground. What Red Cloud knew then was that he had won his war, that he had given up nothing whatever to get what he wanted from the other side, that he had forced the United States government and army out of his territory. That here, at long last, his people had stopped the devastating advance of the white man.

He would be right for about ten years. That, now, is what we know. But that also is the significance of the story. And that is why I write this letter.

If we reconstruct the fort on this site now, we will be as myopic as Colonel Carrington was in originally building it; our focus will be as narrow, our blinders as constricting as his were. And we will be as contemptuously indifferent to his foes as Fetterman was. Except as a symbol, the fort was of no significance whatever; the war for the trail was. And the war ended when the fort burned down. What a travesty to resurrect it now.

Leaving the site empty is the eloquent way, and the only accurate way, to convey its significance. The monument raised years ago on the hill where Fetterman's troops fell is tribute enough to them, their bravery, their service, their sacrifice. The rest of this great story deserves equal sensitivity.

Remove from the fort site all that even now clutters and trivializes it. Move the visitors' center down close to the road where the potential visitors are. Let the plateau between the Pineys remain empty, windswept, unadorned, a tribute to both soldier and Sioux. Here the latter also bravely served their cause, and sacrificed—and won. For once in this country, let us leave a silent space to attest to something worth remembering in human history.

PART III
History: Points of View

LEARNING FROM LESTER

OFTEN I HAVE BEEN AWED BY PEOPLE WHO RUN local historical societies. They tend to be dedicated, energetic, independent, and provocative—one might even say indomitable, exhausting, hard-headed, and cantankerous. Take, for example, Lester.

I first met Lester in the early 1980s when I was director of the American Association for State and Local History, headquartered in Nashville. An invitation arrived in the mail one day from the Old Hickory Historical Society, down in Hickory County, Tennessee, to come give a speech on the subject "Hard Times for History: Is There Hope?" I accepted, and when the time came, I traveled a long stretch of interstate highway, then took a right on a gravel county road. Before long its left fork became the main street of the Hickory County seat. There I located the fire hall, where the meeting was to convene.

I immediately found myself taken in tow by Lester F. Brubaker, president and general manager of the historical society. From him, in fact, I had received the invitation. From him also I had received in advance a check for my travel expenses, accompanied by a recently audited financial statement, apparently as assurance that the historical society was solvent.

"Glad you're here, son." That was the first thing Lester said to me. Then he added: "I've dragooned most of the county in and we're ready to hear what you've got to say." Indeed, the place was packed so tight that the fire engine had been parked outside for the evening to make room.

Lester appeared to be a man of some sixty-five years. He had salt-and-pepper hair, cut short like a Marine's. He wore a dark herringbone suit to match. And he had an attitude about him that was southernly genteel but not long-suffering. It turned out, as I soon learned, that the

77

F in Lester F. Brubaker stood for Fillmore. That had been the maiden name of his mother, who had northern antecedents. Through her, he was a direct descendent of President Millard Fillmore and proud of it. That was the same president, of course, to whom the prominent American historian Allan Nevins has referred in print as "the dim and forgotten Fillmore." I had at home a recording of political ditties entitled, "Sing Along with Millard Fillmore." Nonetheless I said politely to Lester, after I learned of his connection, "He wasn't a bad president, really."

"The hell he wasn't," Lester promptly rejoined. "Let's not fudge our historical facts, son. What he was was a reasonably fair lawyer." That, it turned out, was what Lester had been before he took over the historical society. As he led me to the podium, he muttered in my ear, "By the way, I hope you're not going to denounce genealogy tonight. A lot of us got into this history business by wondering if we had anything other than no-account ancestors." I assured him that genealogy would get no guff from me. Then I delivered myself of my wisdom, which began as follows:

"This is a tough time for history, for those of us whose social responsibility it is to save and care for and use the historical resources of this country, for those of us who preserve and study the museum artifacts and the documentary records and the historic sites and structures that constitute the indispensable and irreplaceable evidence of American's past."

Suddenly, Lester was at my elbow.

"Not too much poetry, son," he whispered in my ear with his head turned away from the audience. "Let's get down to business."

"Right," I said, not a little disconcerted. I skipped a couple of pages before continuing:

"Heretofore help has been available to us from several federal agencies." I then described the Historic Preservation Fund in the Department of the Interior, the National Endowment for the Humanities and the National Endowment for the Arts, the Institute of Museum Services, the National Archives and its subsidiary, the National Historical Publications and Records Commission, and—but all of a sudden Lester audibly piped up:

"Hang all that history-this and humanities-that stuff, son. Tell us about CETA. We used to have two CETA workers right here at the Old

Hickory Historical Society, and now we can't seem to get them any more."

CETA stood for Comprehensive Employment Training Act. While it lasted, it was a federal program for putting people to work. It especially benefited social welfare and cultural service organizations that could not afford to pay people while training them. I now think it may have been the most valuable direct help for small historical societies and museums provided by the government since the WPA in the New Deal era. But I did not realize that then. So I told Lester that my point was going to be that all federal assistance programs were in jeopardy, and if I could continue my speech, I would try to suggest what could be done about it.

"Good idea. Proceed," Lester said.

Turning once more to the audience, I said: "All federal assistance programs are in jeopardy. The Congress is under pressure to reduce deficits by cutting budgets. Historical societies that in future hope to continue to get federal grants will need to compete harder. For one thing, they will need to show a broad base of public support. For example, they will want to increase the number of their members."

"Members?" Lester's voice again piped up. "Members?"

"Yes," I responded weakly. "Doesn't your historical society have members?"

"Fourteen of them, currently," Lester declared.

Suddenly I sensed an opening for expression of my frustration.

"Mr. Brubaker," I said, hoping my smile conveyed self-assuredness, "I trust you are not excluding people or running an invitation-only club for the socially acceptable."

"Not a bit!" Lester roared back. "Anybody who wants to join us can. We don't care what your family background is, whether you've lived here forever or just moved in. We don't care if you are rich or poor. We don't care about your race, color, religious persuasion, national origin, condition of previous servitude, or sexual preference. You can be a one-legged green Siberian as long as you sign our membership oath before a notary public. It says: 'I will give a minimum of ten hours a week of hard work to this historical society or its museum. Also I will contribute money and will ask others for it. Also I will not miss more than two meetings a year for any reason short of contagious illness or permanent disability. And I will read no fewer than three books a year

out of the historical society library so that I will actually know something abut history and can help identify and keep an eye out for records
and artifacts and sites and buildings that have historical value around
here and need saving and care and use, so help me God.' We are not
interested," Lester concluded, "in having just a bunch of warm bodies
to swell a membership list."

"Well," I said, my smile gone, "surely we can agree on the next point.
Substantial collections," I went on, "will themselves be a key to a historical organization's success in future competition for limited grant
funds. Judging from what you just said, I imagine that half of Hickory
County is by now under your protection and that your museum is
bursting with documents and artifacts."

I paused; I could hear it coming.

"Son," Lester slowly said, "Do you actually understand the field you
are alleging yourself to represent? A historical society does not exist
just to keep stuff. A historical society exists to provide honest judgment
about what's worth keeping and educate its community accordingly.
The first capital acquisition we made when I became president and
general manager was a hayrick so we could haul off an accumulation
that was sitting around at the museum pretending to be history.

"If you have a brain in your head, which seems increasingly open to
question, you are going to help your constituents get through the current financial crunch by telling them this: They should get their history
straight so they can identify the most important, representative, rare,
and useful sites, structures, objects, and records in their communities.
And they should establish priorities for use of however much money is
available. That way, the best stuff will not get lost, and the community's
available cash, however much it is, will get spent first on what needs
and deserves it most. We have standards here, one of which is truth
and another of which is frugality. Don't you understand that?"

"I see," I said.

"Good," Lester said. "But time's passing. Go ahead, continue."

I tried. "Most important," I said, "future success with federal grant-
making agencies will require the avoidance of parochialism. They are
interested in the truly significant. They want to fund activities that illustrate the broad themes of American history in general, that lift local
history into a context that is national."

I knew it; this time Lester was standing.

"Son," he said, "you are indeed one of the muddier thinkers of our time. This is not the Old Hickory Historical Society for American History in General and High Tea. We are not in business to lift up the natives to appreciate broad, vapory themes that may have happened to waft through here historically from time to time.

"I suppose we could tell about the percentage of annual national agricultural production that has come out of our county in the past century, or the extent to which our ethnic groups reflect national immigration patterns, or the theological antecedents of ideas put forth historically by preachers in our pulpits, or how the ideas of the Enlightenment have unfolded through the years over at the county courthouse. But we are not in business to be a bore.

"We are in business, son, to keep track of the history of this place for the people who live in it, because that makes it the most important place in their lives right now. We want to explain specifically how it got the way it is and why, and who did it for better or for worse. The War of Jenkins' Ear and the Prohibition Amendment may have had something to do with it, and they may not. If they did, we'll fit them into local history and not the other way around. People have lived lives here; nobody lives in the War of Jenkins' Ear. Why can't you understand?"

"Well, hell," I blurted out before I could catch myself. "I don't know. I guess I should go shoot myself."

"Also, son," he rejoined, "I notice you don't have any sense of humor. Why don't you just say goodnight to the folks now—you can keep the check—and stay over at my house, and tomorrow I'll show you the museum and take you fishing."

I said goodnight, and everybody, including Lester, clapped mightily. I stayed over. And I went fishing. By then I didn't even care that he caught fourteen fish and I caught none. After all, he knew what he was doing.

Subsequently, however, Lester did help our efforts to keep cultural programs at least alive. He told his district's congressman exactly how to vote, and the congressman did it. They had been law partners, it turned out, and Lester had managed his first campaign. The agencies in which we were interested did in fact survive, and once after a crucial vote, I called Lester as a courtesy to tell him so.

"That's good," was his reply. "But there is big news here as well." I could almost see him grin. "I just got word that our society will get a

81

good-sized grant from the National Endowment for the Humanities, which the First State Bank of Hickory County is going to match!"

"Why you son-of-a-gun," I erupted. "You didn't take any of my advice. How did you wangle that?"

"I'll just tell you," he said cheerily. "My brother-in-law owns the bank. But as for the Humanities Endowment, we got the grant because we put together a no-fat, honest proposal that spelled out our priorities and intentions in plain and persuasive English. Ours was the most sensible, least pretentious proposal they had, and they told me so. Also, however. . . ."

"Yes, Lester?" I said, resigning myself to whatever was coming.

"Also—I figured you would have scared everybody else off by now with your gloom and doom about federal budget cuts, and there would be fewer grant applications to compete with, and it would be just a real good time to get my hand in!"

Well, that is the story. I would guess that down in the archives of the Hickory County Historical Society, my friend Lester goes on trying to figure out why some of the area's pioneers built schools and others stole sheep, and which had the most to do with the current predicaments of that locality.

Yes, of course I made him up. But often in the hot-house of my office, when I was about to bring to full flower some exotic notion about the nature, needs, or requirements of historical activity nationally, I found it useful first to conjure him up in my imagination to ask what a crusty veteran actually out there in the trenches might think? Does this make any real sense? As an antidote to questionable conclusions, Lester proved real enough.

IF BEN FRANKLIN HAD KNOWN ABOUT TEXAS

IN MANY WAYS THE UNITED STATES NOW SEEMS just one big, homogeneous nation. Television sets and chain stores have had a lot to do with that, but in the 20th century, the growth of the federal government and a sense of American nationalism have contributed as well. Correspondingly, the states seem less individual than they did, and also less powerful. "States rights" has become, not without reason, almost a dirty phrase. Moreover, we are so mobile that someone who lives in Delaware today could reside in California tomorrow and do business in Nebraska the day after. Yet every state has its historical society, its archives, and a museum of some kind, usually along with a string of state historic sites, for the simple reason that the states do matter, and in the past certainly have. Public study of their individual histories, through exhibits, historic sites, and publications, can still be rewarding, as I think I can demonstrate if allowed one indulgence: Suppose with me that Ben Franklin knew about Texas.

That is, suppose that Ben Franklin was prescient about all of America, and that, among other future parts of it, the land we now call Texas was brought to his attention one night late in the time of the Constitutional Convention's deliberations. He had set out to seek relaxation in one of those nocturnal visitations against which he counseled in his autobiography, apparently on the basis of considerable experience with their ill effects. But this night, quite a different kind of lady accosted him, an unattractive cackling creature, the leading soothsayer on the American continent at the time:

"Ben," she said, "this Constitutional Convention—there's something that troubles me. This little document all of you are putting together does not just create one big, wonderful democracy, with George Washington keeping everybody in line. Article IV, Section 3, says clearly,

'New states may be admitted by the Congress into this Union,' and Section 4 adds, 'The United States shall guarantee to every state in this Union a republican form of government. . . .'

"Ben," she went on, "you are already trying to force John Adams to like mint juleps. You are already trying to put under one roof the Puritans of Massachusetts, a bunch of Swedes and Dutchmen in Delaware, and the swinging Charlestonians who are regarded with moral horror even by up-countrymen in their own South Carolina. Now you propose to take in states embracing not just territories but even self-styled independent nations—the future Indian Stream Republic in New Hampshire, the Bear Flag Republic in California, and the Kingdom of Hawaii, not to mention the so-called Republic of Texas.

"You are going to try to apply a single, tolerant form of government to everything from the Great American Desert to Seward's Folly. You are going to try to make 'Sooners' and 'Boomers' and Indian chiefs accept the same political system you are imposing on the pirates of Rhode Island.

"And the King's English, if you'll pardon the expression, in which you are composing this incredible document, will be about as intelligible to the Frenchmen of Louisiana, the Spanish of California, the African slaves of Alabama, the Mexicans of New Mexico, and the Alaskan Eskimos as it will be to Geronimo. Half the Oriental miners who eventually will get run out of Montana won't even be able to read their eviction notices. A babble of foreign tongues will be imported here from Europe alone; there will be some fifty different ethnic groups just in Wisconsin, which will even have its own immigration commissioner.

"The former colonies you already have are at each other's throats about one thing and another, but wait until you see the border disputes that fifty states can raise. Wait until you see the southwestern states quarrel over water. Wait until 'Bleeding Kansas.' Wait until the Civil War. Ben, that's what this system of semi-sovereign states will come to.

"And what are you going to do when a bunch of Kentuckians want to form a state of Transylvania, when parts of Idaho and Washington and what-not think they ought to be the state of Columbia, when Colorado miners dream up Jefferson Territory? Part of Tennessee, you may as well know, will want admission as the state of Franklin, in honor of you!

"Consider just the logistics of it, Ben. It's going to take highways to

84

wed Kentucky to the Union. It's going to take steamboats truly to get
Minnesota in. It's going to take railroads for California, and airplanes
for Hawaii. Are you prepared to invent all that?

"Moreover, in one way or another, every state and territory is going
to squirm and fidget and fight. Louisiana and California are going to
battle the nation itself for tideland oil. Texas will embroil you constantly in disputes with Mexico. And no matter what President Taft says,
Arizonans will hold out for the recall-of-judges provision in their constitution as stubbornly as the Utah Mormons will insist on polygamy.
Ben, it's going to be scary out there.

"Louisiana will persist in having parishes instead of counties and
may never entirely give up the Napoleonic Code. Nebraska will thumb
its nose at two-house legislatures. Minnesota will have two slightly differing constitutions, both at the same time. Mississippi will subordinate
its executive and judicial branches to its legislature, but other states will
not. Arizonans will try a perfect state of nature for a while, with no government, no taxes, no public debt, and no politics, except for the sort
practiced by vigilantes. The legal requirement for divorce in South
Carolina will be air fare to Nevada. And loyalties to all those state enti-
ties will be as great as Lee's to Virginia. Wait until you see what hap-
pens to the Union because of that!

"As for democracy and republican forms of government within the
states, copper kings someday will buy up the newspapers of Montana,
insurance companies will dominate New York, and railroads will run
California. They'll argue in Tennessee about Boss Crump and in Illinois about Mayor Daley and in Louisiana about Huey Long forever.
Only some questionable ballot counting will keep a goat-gland doctor
out of the governorship of Kansas, and Georgia will elect a purveyor of
hot grits and axe handles.

"And Texas, Ben, Texas—you think the nation will be in sad shape
when public life degenerates into such factions and parties as Whigs
and Democratic Republicans. Texas, Ben, is going to have 'Woodpeck-
er Republicans' and 'Jaybird Democrats,' among other exotic varieties.
And Texas will experiment with camels and county-option liquor laws,
and go so far as to put a tax on traveling salesmen and even on us for-
tune tellers!

"Ben, don't you think you better reconsider this whole thing?"

Well, that did give Franklin pause. But not for long. After due reflection, he replied simply, "What other choice do we have? Freeze the Allegheny frontier? Turn down all offers for the Louisiana Purchase, no matter how ridiculously low the price? Why, I doubt that even a strict constructionist like Tom Jefferson would do that! And haven't we now just demonstrated to King George that you can't govern an empire on this continent on tyrannical principles? No, we shall have states, and they will become part of the great American political experiment, with whatever chances that involves.

"Moreover, you likely do the states a great injustice. There is room within the republic for differences, for experimentation. It is even conceivable that at certain times the nation may learn, negatively and positively, from certain states. I predict that, if anything, the new western states may be more nationalistic in outlook, and more democratic in spirit, than the former colonies. I'd not be surprised if an Alabama, Missouri, Indiana, or Illinois would extend the ballot to all adult white males before New England does; that a Wyoming would first give women suffrage; that a Georgia or Kentucky would enable eighteen-year-olds to vote; that states such as an Oklahoma would show us the effects of the long ballot, the elected judiciary, and the referendum and initiative; that a Montana would go so far as to send a female to the Congress; that from an Oregon or a Wisconsin, as well as from New York and Massachusetts, we would learn a lot about social legislation and labor law; that a state of Wisconsin might in time become a veritable political laboratory studied by other states and the nation.

"As for Texas, my dear, which you so demean, I suggest that a further look in your crystal ball might show a period when that state provides national leadership through progressive legislation on railroads, antitrust, insurance, homesteading, and public lands for higher education. As for the tall-tale telling and wheeler-dealerism you worryingly anticipate, well, I'm a bit of a shrewd operator with a love of a good story myself!

"Additionally, why can't the states serve the nation, as well as themselves, as training grounds for political leadership? An Ohio alone could easily give us eight (albeit less than immortal) presidents: Grant, Hayes, Garfield, McKinley, Taft, Harding, and the two Harrisons. More impressive, an Illinois might give us a Lincoln; a Wilson could cut his political and administrative teeth in New Jersey; and various Roosevelts might develop their skills in New York. Strong leaders, if not totally lovable ones, might even come from Texas—Colonel House, Speaker Sam Rayburn, John Nance Garner, LBJ.

"The states will make a mixed and controversial record, I'm sure; so will the nation. Our revolution may have begun in Boston and Philadelphia, but in effect it will extend someday to Sacramento, Juneau, and Honolulu. The states could eventually lose much of their sovereignty and variety, but people will still live lives and make laws within them, and each will have some influence on the whole. Over time each will have a significant story as well as an interesting one. They will all be part of our experiment with democracy, and each in its own right, therefore, will well be worth evaluation by historians and the scrutiny of the history-minded public."

There is no actual evidence, of course, that Ben Franklin said anything like that. But a man of his perspicacity certainly could have. And I submit that he would have been quite right.

TEN STRANGE WAYS TO CELEBRATE A CENTENNIAL

BIRTHDAYS ARE WONDERFUL; WE ALL HAVE THEM. For one whole day every year, we are treated to an astonishing experience: People go out of their way to be nice to us. Family members who normally growl as they get up in the morning give us breakfast in bed. Business associates who tried to do us in the day before take us to lunch or dinner. Relatives from whom we hear nothing for months on end send us congratulatory cards or telegrams, or even call on the phone. We also receive presents, some of them wrapped in colored paper and decorated with ribbons and bows. At the least, we have ice cream and cake—and a wish that is certified to come true if we can still blow out all the candles in one breath. In time, people become nice enough even to quit trying to find room on the cake for a candle for every one of our years.

We know full well the psychological point of all this. We get our day as a testimonial to our importance, a celebration of our survival, a tribute to our worth in the world. And so it is with the birthdays of our nation, states, cities, counties, and towns. Those, however, we call centennials (bi-, ter-, quadri-, quin-, etc., depending on how old our place is). On those anniversaries, we salute ourselves as groups, often with banquets instead of lunches, speeches in place of cards or telephone calls, fireworks in lieu of ordinary candles, and, by way of presents, something we call history.

There seems no end to the creativity with which we concoct presentations to ourselves under that exalted name. Smith Center is a hundred years old? Wonderful! Let's consecrate, let's hallow its history, let's get all the men in the Chamber of Commerce to grow beards and wear cocked hats (substitute coonskin, ten-gallon, or even war bonnet, depending on what region of the country Smith Center is in and our degree of high spirit or insensitivity). Also, let's have an essay contest on patriotism for the high school students. Then let's get some old-time fiddlers for a country dance (square, barn, quadrille, polka, or even waltz, depending on regional location and our degree of pride in ethnic particularity). And on Founder's Day, let's get everybody to dress up like (fill in: patriots/pioneers/cavalry) and re-enact the Battle of Indian Bluff.

In the midst of such discussions these days, however, some wearisomely conscientious soul is likely to interject: "Shouldn't we also take on some project that is, you know, serious?"

Well of course. We then come to the sober realization that the old train station needs saving, that a marker should go up on the site of the first European settlement, that a local history book should be written, and above all else that the community should create—yes—a history museum. Thus will Smith Center give itself on its birthday a more permanent kind of commemoration.

Sound familiar so far? Something along those lines has occurred throughout the 1970s and 1980s all across the country. The bicentennials of the American Revolution and the Constitution have made us even more conscious of historical anniversaries than usual. Further encouragement has come from a spate of state centennials, including six in the Northwest in 1989 and 1990 (the Dakotas, Montana, Washington, Idaho, and Wyoming). Economic pressure to attract tourists and sell relocating industries on the glories of our localities also is leading thousands of communities to commemorate their beginnings with considerable flair. And who says they should not? Indeed, I wish to offer some suggestions of unusual, if not extraordinary, ways for doing so.

First, however, let me speculate about what is likely to happen in Smith Center if it undertakes even the most modest of those "serious" possibilities for commemorating its history—setting up, say, a marker on the site of the city's original settlement. If we are the committee to carry out that project in Smith Center, what must we do? First, obviously, we need to find out what, where, and when the first settlement was. That should be easy enough.

We begin with a trip to the local historical society. Smith Center has, let us suppose, a lively one, which presents a speaker to its members once a month and provides them with a newsletter. The society's director has some answers to our questions, of course, but they seem rather conjectural. If the city is going to invest in a permanent, metal marker, intended to identify the settlement site and its significance forever, prudence compels us to seek documentation. Is there any?

"Well," says the director, "there's the town charter and some related documents in an old safe back here where we keep the artifacts we've been collecting in hope of someday opening a real museum. But we haven't had occasion to get the documents out for some time."

Unfortunately, the old iron safe—clearly an antique itself—is so rusted shut that when we finally find it the combination simply doesn't work. Our suggestion that we use a blowtorch at first horrifies the historical society director. But the documents might as well be burned up as impounded in perpetuity out of sight, so why not take a chance on drastic action? The blowtorch works, and we withdraw a file of documents that look wonderfully historic. Unfortunately, they pertain to Smith Center's incorporation and not much else.

"Well," suggests the director, "you might try the public library, to which we've made a more or less permanent loan of the books and manuscripts we once collected about the town's beginnings."

The librarian, fortunately, knows exactly where the local history shelf is in the public library stacks, and takes us there. Unfortunately, the card catalogue tells us nothing about what is in each box, nor is there any other index. As we start a laborious search, the old paper threatens to crumble in our hands. "The old books will be dust before long, too," the librarian informs us. "The kind of paper used particularly between 1870 and 1900 won't hold up much longer." Several days later we manage to find a couple of items in the handwriting of original settlers, who describe a small trading post on the riverbank as the first settlement—some solid evidence at last! They give differing dates, however, for when it was established, and we find it hard to figure out from their recollections exactly what it looked like, or where precisely in the current downtown area the log structure stood.

The librarian's suggestion that land titles, deeds, and related documents might contain clues takes us to the county courthouse. The county clerk is cooperative, saying, "All that old stuff, best as I recollect, is up in the courthouse attic or down in the basement; our files here are overflowing just with fairly recent records."

The basement sounds slightly more accessible, so we start there. We find files stashed in cardboard boxes and garbage bags, but they yield nothing pertinent to our quest; earlier files turn up in an old bathtub over by the boiler room. We have to handle them carefully, so moldy have they become, but in a few days we do get a clearer indication, from studying plats among the other records, where the first structure stood. We don't try the attic at all; half the records up there already have faded or become too brittle from the heat to touch, and rodents seem to have found their corners good to eat.

"Have you thought of trying the newspaper's files?" the clerk cheerily inquires. "Might be some historical reminiscences about first settlement in the early editions."

The publisher welcomes us with equal good cheer and lets us spend all the time we want with the old newspaper files in his conference room. He knows right where the oldest issues are. The only problem is that old newsprint was made out of an even cheaper wood pulp than the other paper materials we have been examining. "Hmm," the publisher says, blowing the dust away, "I'm afraid they're pretty yellow and crumbly now."

Nonetheless, we turn up a readable and thorough eyewitness account of the first settlement. It furnishes enough detail to resolve the date difficulty, and it pinpoints more closely the exact site. How about photographs? Do the newspaper files have any pictures going back far enough to show that first building, which might have remained intact for some time as the city grew up around it? Joyfully, we discover that prints still exist from the newspaper's first use of photography. They have faded considerably already, but in one photo we are able to make out that first structure still standing. So it did survive quite a while.

Then we get another break. The reporter whose beat includes hospitals has overheard us. "Hey, if you go soon, you can ask Mrs. So-and-So about all that. She's the granddaughter of one of the town's founders. Don't know how long she's going to live, but. . . ."

She looks as fragile, there in the hospital bed, as the old documents we've been examining, but nothing is wrong with her memory or her speech, and she is delighted to pass some time telling us about the old days. The log structure, she insists, never was torn down. It was "improved;" that is, it was plastered over and incorporated into a new, larger structure. "You know the one," she says. "It was part of that corner building that sat vacant for so long and then burned down last winter after some kids got in. Remember?"

We do remember, and a sudden sinking feeling fills our hearts. Up until a half-year ago, had we known, we could have identified not only the site but preserved the original settlement structure. Now we must be content with tape recording her recollections of it. Thank goodness we discovered her in time! She even gives us an additional idea for marking the settlement site: "Out there in the far corner of City Park, there used to be a statue of the town's founder. I think the WPA people made it during the Depression. Nobody's paid much attention to it since. Why don't you move it to the riverfront site?"

It soon becomes evident why we didn't know about the statue. It still stands, more or less, but in a remote corner of the park, away from the pathways and picnic benches, half hidden by hedges that have grown up in the area. The city engineer comes to look at it with us.

"I like your idea about moving it downtown," he says. "But I don't know if we can move it safely, not without a lot of expert repair work first. See what the weather has done to it here? And over here, these cracks look like somebody tried to get it off the pedestal.

"By the way," he adds, "when the demolition crew leveled the shell of that old building after the fire, their bulldozer stirred up the ground and they found some old bottles and other stuff that might be from the original trading post. You might want to check over at the maintenance depot to see if any of that's still around."

"Great," we respond. "Maybe we, too, can dig for artifacts at the site?"

"Afraid not," he tells us. "The owner paved it over a couple of months ago to use as a parking lot."

Thus several months after our search began—a search for a few simple facts to put on a permanent historical marker—we finally report back to the centennial committee. Yes, we now know the exact site and the precise date of the first settlement in Smith Center. Also, if artifacts are wanted for the new museum that is also proposed for commemorating the centennial, several old glass jugs can be retrieved from the maintenance depot, where a couple of crewmen have amused themselves by making them into lamp stands. But at least the artifacts exist, and are in no worse condition than anything else that pertains to the town's early history.

Our job done, we look forward to a fine time in Smith Center on the day we observe the 100th anniversary of its founding. There all of us will be, downtown at the site by the river, standing at the corner of the paved, empty parking lot, raising a big, expensive, durable metal marker. Wearing our coonskin hats or whatever, we will listen to the mayor speak of how far our city has come in so short a time. And certainly it has. Simultaneously, of course, the documents at the historical society and the manuscripts at the library and the records at the county courthouse and the newsprint and photographs at the newspaper office will go on crumbling, molding, yellowing, fading, and disappearing into attics and basement storage bins. Simultaneously as well, obituaries will record the loss of living memories of historical experience, vandals will try the doors of more old buildings, statues will go on deteriorating in the park, and artifacts will continue disintegrating in the ground beneath our feet. But by gosh we will not have neglected, in this, our anniversary year, to pay tribute to our great history!

The point, I trust, is by now clear. But what to do about it? There is an alternative to the kind of commemoration I have described above. Let me propose my ten ways to celebrate a centennial.

One: Make a survey; find out where the community's most valuable historical things are and what condition they are in.

Two: Organize, preserve, and regularly update that information for future reference.

Three: Establish priorities for preserving each kind of historical material.

Four: Get professional help to preserve the material worth saving in original form.

Five: Photograph, photocopy, microfilm, tape record, or otherwise document the rest of what is valuable.

Six: Set up a historical-hazard alert system to let the community know when a valuable building, site, collection, or set of records is in danger.

Seven: Lobby government officials to adopt records management programs so that important documents won't get lost.

Eight: Arrange now with leaders of community organizations to preserve records and artifacts from the present that one day will have historical value.

Nine: Arrange with other communities to divide up responsibilities for saving things pertaining to common histories and to share collections, exchange exhibits, and otherwise avoid expensive duplication.

Ten: Then have a centennial party you can really enjoy because the irreplaceable evidence of your community's history will be—Oh happy day!—secure.

GREAT HISTORIANS I HAVE KNOWN

The L.O.L.

HOW NICE TO SEE TODAY, IN ONE OF THE TOWNS
out on the plains where I grew up, a fine historical museum, professionally administered. Yet I continue to think back fondly of what the
museum used to be, and of the person who ran it. I suppose some people might make fun of her as what professionals call an "L.O.L"—a little old lady in tennis shoes. If she wore them, I never noticed, because
I was too fascinated by things in the museum that she kept.

"Kept" is too mild a word; many of the documents and artifacts belonged to her. They had come down to her as a direct descendant of
one of the town's founders, and I gather she had scrounged around and
badgered people to give her other old things that she felt belonged
with the collection. Once she got them, she put the papers into an iron
safe and the artifacts into locked glass cases in a room upstairs in the
public library building. That was the museum. Every year, sixth grade
classes from the town's schools were trooped up there in a kind of hol-
iday spirit to find out something about their local history.

In my mind's eye, I can still see her now—a short, wiry woman with
sharp eyes and a lot of names, dates and tales on her tongue pertaining
to pioneer triumphs and tribulations. Much of it she apparently
learned at the knees of her own forebears, whose town it had been, lit-
erally. When she spoke, so it seemed to me, history itself was speaking,
such was her authority. And hearing her was to know what the phrase
"possessing knowledge" really meant; she had it and would share it, but
it was clearly, personally hers.

Some of the museum pieces did acknowledge another owner or
donor. I remember one exotic example in particular, a small statue,
maybe four feet tall, like a cigar-store Indian, only this was a Japanese
warrior in battle dress from some early era. A fierce-looking fellow, he

was, and so wonderfully lifelike that sixth graders, wanting to see if he could or would move, found it irresistible to give him a poke. Around his neck she had placed two signs, or, as museum professionals now would call them, labels. As best I remember, one sign said something like this: "Gift of Mrs. J. Jones, who brought it back from Tokyo in 1923, by boat."

The other said: "Japanese warrior. Do not poke."

I have some recollection of the quickness with which she could interrupt a history lecture to stop one of us school kids from fiddling with things in the museum collection. She seemed equally decisive, I was to learn in the course of some research of my own later, in correcting historians. A staunch Republican and temperance woman, she wrote in the margins of old history books that references to the consumption of whiskey in the town's early days were errors attributable to "Democrat opinion."

Obviously history was no abstract study to her, which is what most makes her memorable to me now. She was custodian of our town's portion of it, and as such, she would battle both the mischievous and the misinformed. In local history work, she herself was our pioneer. Without her saving and collecting and preserving, little that was tangible would remain as evidence that we had a history. Her jealousy, her tenacity, her care conveyed a belief that was clear: History was a possession. And it was one we could not afford to lose.

The Man Who Knew

A TENNESSEE FARMER SURPRISED ME BY APPEARING unannounced one afternoon in my office at the American Association for State and Local History. At least that is what he appeared to be. He wore a suit coat over a pair of overalls, and his thin hair showed a line where his cap came down over it. His fingers were thick from manual work, and his speech was blunt. He had come to ask questions about starting a history museum. But there were some things that "experts" were not going to tell him, it soon became clear. Chiefly, they were not going to tell him not to do it.

Over the years, it turned out, he had been amassing a huge collection of farm equipment and household utensils, some of them from as far back as the turn of the century, including much horsedrawn machinery. How old he himself was, I could not tell. But he was old enough to know how log cabins were made and what they were like to live in, because he grew up in one. He knew. Did I know, he asked, what it was like in Tennessee on a farm before rural electrification? Did I know?

What he wanted to do, he explained, was assemble all that machinery on an old-time farm, and put all those utensils in log cabins, and show it all to school kids, so that they would know what things were like then. He wanted them to know. He recognized that some modern contrivances would be necessary—drinking fountains, toilets, a security system, equipment for what museums call indoor climate control. But he would install such devices to be hidden so that the kids would not see anything that had not been there in historical reality.

"I don't like nothing that ain't authentic," he said. He knew what was authentic. He knew.

As for the farm equipment, people gave it to him when others didn't show proper interest in it, he said. Mostly, it was old machinery he had restored to "mint condition," he said; ancient machinery but still "ready to go in the field." He knew how to maintain and operate it. He knew how it had been and still could be used.

I was unsure quite how to advise him. I could refer him to sources of expertise on how to conserve artifacts, how to exhibit them, how to "interpret" them, to use the professional jargon. I tried to talk him into offering his collection to a professionally staffed museum. But I think he sensed that the attitudes of professionals in the field might be different from his. Their interest in his objects might be primarily aesthetic. They might like the design or charm or rarity of something, or they might admire it as representative of a certain historical style.

Obviously, he admired the old things, too. But not for their feeling or look or place in history. He prized them because they would still operate. History was something more than change over time to him. It inhered in the use of things. He knew how his objects were used and how life was when people were using them. And the more we talked the more evident it became that he could not bear the thought that new generations might forget.

97

I saw no more of him after his visit that day, and I never heard what became of his plans and his collection. But I have not viewed an agricultural exhibit since without thinking of him. His sense of history was personal and powerful. It never occurs to most of us that humanity might simply forget an entire era if we don't provide for it. But he knew. He knew.

The Virgin's Lift

THIS HISTORIAN I DID NOT PERSONALLY KNOW well, but he is a well-known art historian, and I should credit him by name for the wonderful thing he did. Richard Brettell figured out how to restore "the lift of the Virgin."

At the time, Brettell was curator of European art at the Art Institute of Chicago. The Virgin is Mary, mother of Jesus, in El Greco's famed painting of her "assumption." The painting is among those that have made the Art Institute one of the seven or eight greatest all-around art museums in America. The painting is so inseparable from the Art Institute's identity that the staff refers to it as "one of our icons." In it, Mary is ascending from the Earth up to Heaven on a crescent moon. She looks magnificent. But Richard Brettell saw that there was something wrong with her "lift."

Curators at the Art Institute had long known there was something wrong with the painting. For generations, guides had pointed to the painting's edges and said to visitors, "You see the foot of that angel? El Greco didn't paint that foot." El Greco painted the Virgin in the 15th century for an altarpiece in Spain from which it was subsequently removed. By the time it came to the Art Institute in 1906, someone hidden in the intervening historical mist had added roughly eight inches to each side, apparently to make the painting fit a frame too large for the original. No one at the Art Institute did anything about it. Everyone came to accept the additions as "natural," Brettell said, until he couldn't stand it anymore.

"The more I looked at it, the more disturbed I was by the addition of the eight inches on the sides, because what it does is lessen the sense of vertical thrust, of physical urgency, about the picture—the lift of the Virgin is much less emphasized." He did not take up shears and cut off the offending edges. "We couldn't do that; the additions had become part of the painting's history," he said. But he hid them within a new frame—a specially commissioned, altarlike frame—built with great care to fit the original painting and enhance it properly. He also moved the painting to one of the main galleries, a renovated room with new lighting, where one could see it as one mounted the Art Institute's grand central staircase.

There Brettell viewed it ecstatically. Visitors now, he said, can fully experience "the urgency of the Virgin's lift, her assumption into glory, into Heaven, which particularly in a room that is skylit is wonderful! And the light that will shine upon her will not be lateral light, as it was, but light from above, and she will rise into it!"

And so she does. And such is another of the mysterious ways in which historians work.

My Friend

MY FRIEND LIVES IN ONE OF THOSE SMALL TOWNS that harassed urbanites often dream of—a town of fewer than a thousand people in which time and history seem to have stood still, a town of old white houses, lawns full of leaves, and so much peace and quiet that my friend there genuinely looks forward every day to the fire siren that announces noon.

"You want to do what?" my friend said on the phone.

"I want to come down for the weekend," I repeated. "I need to get away from it all. Besides, you promised if I did come some day, you'd give me a tour of all the local history."

It would be all right to come, he allowed, as long as I didn't arrive before Saturday. On Friday he had to take his Uncle Dan to the hospital for an examination. It seems that Uncle Dan had been having conversations again with articles in his clothes closet. He had accused them of hiding there until nightfall to steal his collection of duck decoys.

When I arrived Saturday morning, my friend suggested a walk. In fact it was imperative, because his Aunt June would wonder where her mail was and get upset if he didn't appear with it at the usual time. She wouldn't trust him with the key to her post office box, so he had to ask for her mail at the counter. He carried her mail in a little sack because she also didn't trust him to carry it loose without losing it. Later, we would also make a trip to the grocery store to get vanilla extract for his Aunt Julia. On the way out I said:

"Wasn't that clerk the same woman who gave you Aunt June's mail at the post office?"

"She works quite a few places around town," he said.

At his suggestion, I waited on the street while he made his deliveries—waited under a great, shimmering golden-green willow. A bird chirped. A cat ambled by. How idyllic, I thought. I had ample time to think because it was a good half-hour before my friend came out.

"Aunt June is something of a talker," he explained, "and she keeps well up on all local matters."

On the way back, he gave me a tour. First, there was a big, white house, which my friend explained had been a couple's wedding present from parents on both sides; one family was in real estate and the other owned the lumber yard. In fact, they built it next door to the parents of the bride, whose mother insisted on a connecting walkway in back, in case of trouble. A cupola on the house had long ago blown away, and my friend didn't know how the marriage had turned out.

"Now here's the creek," my friend stopped to point out. "It used to flood the town, and people would come from the bigger town up the road, higher up, to see our flood. That always made my Uncle Rudy mad. He used to say he was going to go outside in the water and splash around and act like he was drowning to see how they liked that. But he never did."

We reached a grassy square, which my friend explained was East Park, in the town's East End. West Park was in the West End, where the more well-off citizens once lived. East Park had a Civil War memorial in it, with twenty-some names on it of soldiers who had fallen in the Union cause. Only soldiers from the East End were listed on it, however, because the people in the East End thought if the West Enders had any soldiers to honor they ought to pay for a monument of their own. Later, there also had been a hot argument over whether to tear down the gas plant in the East End, after many people began to use electricity, particularly in the West End. "Feelings got pretty strong," my friend said. "Finally there had to be a referendum before the West End won."

As we reached Main Street "downtown," my friend explained that the citizens traditionally had split up also among five religious denominations and two car dealerships. The Irish Catholics tended to buy Fords, which they got fixed at his Great Uncle Pat's garage, whereas the German and English Protestants of various denominations usually bought Chevies, which the rival garage repaired. Great Aunt Sheila, Great Uncle Pat's wife, never forgave the other garage for advertising back in the 1950s that its new heating system spared mechanics and patrons from draftiness in bad weather—an invidious comparison, she thought.

My friend also pointed out to me the sites of five bars, corresponding in number to the religious denominations. Immediately across the street from the Catholic church, he said, was one where the men used to stop before midnight mass, while the women went ahead. It was always interesting later, he said, to watch the men try to make it up to the communion rail.

The generally acknowledged town drunk (though there had been several eligible contenders) had died some years ago, he said. "I guess Aunt Jennifer could claim the title now. She's seventy-four now. She likes to get swishing drunk and go out and tell certain people how they are ruining the town."

My friend next pointed out the sites of several disasters. "There's where the Valhalla Hotel stood," he said. "I never saw it. My mother watched it burn down. Then up there, on that road over the railroad tracks, the grocery deliveryman in his truck got hit by a train once. All of us came over from the high school to see the squashed vegetables and blood."

Several of his relatives had left town at various times. One uncle had been president of a bank that hadn't survived the Depression. He had then gone to California with a female teller. Also long departed was Uncle Herman, who had worked in a drygoods store. Herman's wife got mad once at the town newspaper when it reported that the store's proprietor had left town for a few days, but "Herman and the sales girls are carrying on."

I noticed a nice old building, squarish, with a belfry that contained a big clock. A sign on the building said, "Library."
"Is that really the library?" I asked.
"It used to be," my friend said. "They put that tower up on the roof when I was a kid. Some civic-minded man left money for it in his will. I don't know why he thought the library should have a clock and bells. Also, I don't know why the town jail was downstairs. But we used to go there sometimes to see the town drunk."

Soon we turned off Main Street again towards the home that my friend shares with his Aunt Jillian. "I think she'll be back now from playing bridge," he said. "She plays most of the afternoon. She and the others chat a while, but then when they play they don't talk so much. She generally wins quite a few quarters."

"That was quite a tour," I said. "I never before heard local history recounted quite like that."

"Actually," said my friend, "you can find it just as well in Sigmund Freud's *Civilization and its Discontents.* Especially the section about how people historically seem to take hostile sides no matter how small the groups. Anyway, we better go in now. Aunt Jillian will be mad if she thinks we stayed so long at Aunt June's that we're late for lunch. Also, she's eager to know whether you agree, after seeing this place, that the town up the road is ugly and insufferable."

Jimmie

JIMMIE LIVES IN A TOWN IN ALABAMA. I WON'T SAY where, except that it isn't Montgomery, and that is its big problem. In Montgomery, there are lots of old plantation houses still around, and a sense of social aristocracy that others in Alabama envy. So others naturally go looking for what might have been plantation houses in their own areas and exhibit them as historic houses to show that aristocracy existed where they live, too.

One such place exhibited as an antebellum mansion is, indeed, a splendid house. Jimmie told me a Yankee businessman—some odd entrepreneur from the East Coast—bought it early in the 20th century and put a lot of money into making it grand. Indeed, Jimmie said, a professional preservationist once recommended that it be interpreted as an outstanding example of 1920s taste. But 1920s taste doesn't get you anywhere with the aristocracy of Alabama. And so the people who have preserved this historic house, but who aren't fortunate enough to have it in Montgomery, keep its columns well painted and maintain a formal garden around it and tell visitors it was a plantation house.

"Why of course it was," Jimmie's grandmother told me at lunch when I was visiting. "Don't you listen to that Jimmie. He wasn't even born."

The central part of the mansion, at least, was indeed built before the War of Northern Aggression. And some interesting people of local significance did originally live in it, Jimmie told me. But they were farmers, not Scarlett O'Hara. They may have had a slave or two, not hundreds. Mostly they raised goats along with some cotton and corn. And it has been difficult to know quite what to say about those facts—about Yankees and goats—in the interpretive program of the great "plantation house."

"Now Jimmie," Jimmie's grandmother said, "let's just not worry about a few little old goats."

Jimmie, however, had to worry about such things, because the county's historical society, which was housed in the old mansion, had hired him as its first real director. He had completed work in history and then in museum studies at a university. He had done considerable research on the house.

"I showed the board my research," Jimmie told me. "I told them that there probably was no real plantation here. They told me that there probably was."

"Oh Jimmie—he's so young," his grandmother interrupted to say to me. "You know how young people are. Would you like some tea with your lunch? Or some more bourbon?"

Jimmie had found an ally, however, in a great aunt of his named Eloise who was on the board and thought it just a hoot that the old mansion had been nothing before the Civil War but a goat farm. However, she was not of much practical help.

Once she declared gleefully at a board meeting, "It's just like y'all in this town to get caught in a lot of nonsense. I move we tear the damned thing down."

"At least Aunt Eloise agrees we shouldn't fib," Jimmie argued to his grandmother at lunch.

"Oh that Eloise," his grandmother responded. "She's such a bird!"

"What's a bird?" I asked Jimmie later.

"It's kind of hard to explain," he said. "It's sort of a regional term that you have to live here a while to understand. It's sort of a cross between being ridiculous and crazy but also inconsequential. When applied to someone like Aunt Eloise, it means you are just supposed to laugh and pay no attention."

But Jimmie had nonetheless slowly, carefully, quietly begun to restore the house and grounds to the way they were in the 1920s when the place was made elegant by a Yankee businessman. It didn't mean there couldn't be flowers; it just meant they would be of different kinds and in different places. It didn't mean there couldn't be paint and nice furniture. It just meant the paint wouldn't always be gleaming white and the furniture would be more modern. Of course, members of the board did ask some questions when they came to the mansion.

"Are you sure this is the kind of wallpaper they had before the War, Jimmie?"

"No'm," Jimmie would reply. "I'm not sure. We don't really know what kind of wallpaper was in this house before the Civil War."

"Oh. Well, it's nice enough. But that old antique table we had that belonged to Mr. DuVall's great-grandfather before the War. What became of that? Didn't it used to sit right here?"

"Yes'm," Jimmie would reply. "But we took it out to be fixed. It may take quite a while."

"Oh. Well, it still looks like pretty nice furniture you brought in here. But didn't we have a garden laid out all nice and symmetrical once?"

"Yes'm," Jimmie would reply. "But it was very expensive to keep up that way. This is just as beautiful, don't you think? And it saves all of you on the board a lot of money."

"Oh, yes, well, now that you mention it, Jimmie, it does look very nice. Historical authenticity is important, but there are practical limits, aren't there? We're sure glad you aren't being a purist about the place."

"Yes'm," Jimmie said.

Afterwards, I said to him: "It looks like eventually you are going to get them to accept this place for what really was its significant period. Congratulations."

"Thanks," Jimmie said. "But actually, I'm not so sure it's right. Sometimes I think I'd like to restore the place back to when it was a goat farm. Tell what life actually was like here—a neglected part of our state's story. But," he sighed, "I'd have a hard time getting my board to keep saving the place at all. One way or another, I guess, we always seem to have to fix up history."

"You mean the Yankee businessman didn't give the house its greatest significance?" I asked.

Jimmie shrugged and replied, "He was just a bird."

The Bicentennial State Historians

LET ME CONCLUDE WITH A SIMPLE TRIBUTE TO A particular group of great historians I have known—51 of them—the authors of a book series entitled *The States and the Nation*, which consists of a volume on each state and the District of Columbia. As managing editor of that series, I had to sign up the authors, encourage and advise them along the way, and supervise the preparation of their manuscripts for press. The American Association for State and Local History produced the series as a project for the Bicentennial of the American Revolution. In retrospect, those days seem full of pride and pleasure, particularly because of the authors' personalities, but at the time, there were exasperations.

For one thing, more than occasionally authors were reluctant to produce manuscripts on deadline. One writer in the series wanted money first with which to visit sites around his state in a rented Ferrari with what he called "attached female footmen." Another was depressed after a torrential rain had struck the historic town he had taken me to visit, caving most of it into an arroyo. Another who, in order to work comfortably, had finally managed to thaw his frozen water pipes with blasts of hot water, assured me he would soon give his manuscript "a dose of the hots." Another delinquent author explained his delay on grounds that he had to go to the Soviet Union, but he would move fast once he got back, he said, for his decks would be clear of everything except getting married.

Then there were the authors who sent me things, usually in lieu of manuscripts. One gave me a red, white, and blue wall-hanging on which she had embroidered: "God Bless George Third!" Others sent a Bicentennial beer can, a bottle of Liberty Ale, a recipe for "Spirit of '76 Salad," and a Bicentennial air-sickness bag. (The last item proved of great use before all the Bicentennial hoopla was over.)

Among the more delinquent authors was one I used to meet at a bar every time I made a trip to his city in hope of prying chapters out of him, as I regularly tried to do. After our first drink, he would always put his hand on my arm and say solemnly, "Jerry, you know, there is no such thing as one martini." It was always interesting, flying home, to try once again to figure out how I had wound up with a huge bar bill and no manuscript.

We did produce the series, and in a relatively short time. Guided by a distinguished editorial board, we started from absolute scratch in the summer of 1973, assembled a small but great staff, signed authors, and had most of the manuscripts in print by 1978, concluding with the rest around the end of the decade. The National Endowment for the Humanities provided grants for the editorial work, and the New York publishing firm of W. W. Norton and Company printed and distributed the books, joining the American Association for State and Local History as copublisher. The books individually and as a series have enjoyed generally good critical reviews, from county newspapers all the way to the *American Historical Review*.

What made the books special, however, was that we sought authors who not only knew well the histories of their states, but who could write well for the general public and who could think well. That is, we did not try to produce a huge, "definitive" history of each state, and we eschewed sheer chronicles of uninterpreted fact—names, dates, events. Instead we asked each author for a relatively short exposition of the historical character of each state, a book-length essay summing up what role the state had taken in the two-hundred-year development of the American nation, an assessment of what seemed significant in the particular experience of its people.

Such a summing up was not easy. One author wrote me in exasperation, "You will forgive me if I grimace a bit at remembering that I have already left out at least twenty facts taught to eighth graders for every one included." But that was ultimately our point—state history has so often been relegated to textbook treatment, bare paragraphs of basic fact made boring by the mandate from education authorities to avoid controversy, prose reduced to a level thought appropriate for the grade in which a state requires that its history be taught.

These historians, too—like those who work in historical societies and museums or who interpret historic sites or their own localities—were for better or worse trying to make sense of human experience for the benefit of the public at large, the layperson, the citizen. That is what puts them all among the greatest historians I have known.

THE GREAT AMERICAN HISTORY: A NOVEL, OR THE STORY ALL AMERICA KNOWS AND LOVES

(With thanks to Horatio Alger, Cecil B. DeMille, John Philip Sousa, and others too numerous to cite)

HEAVE-HO! AT LAST WE ARE OUT UPON THE BROAD waters, under a sunny sky and burgeoning sails, our hopes high. But our hearts are full as we watch our own beloved, sweet, green England receding beyond the stern. So sad it is to know I may never see the dear land of my birth again. Father is here in his black clothes with the great Book to strengthen our resolve, for the Old World has gone wrong now, and freedom-loving, God-fearing men and women must strike out for an unsullied shore, must carve a new commonwealth out of the wilderness in which to purify society.

As night comes on, however, the watchful captain, hobbling peg-legged over the quarterdeck, warns of an impending storm. We gather all in the little hold of the tiny vessel, buoyed by our faith as much as by its creaking timbers, and say our prayers. Our candles sputter as the ship pitches this way and that, and the fierce wind howls through the cracks in the planking. Above, the mainmast sways as though it soon will snap.

"Our Father, we ask only for a new opportunity. Save us, for with Thy Holy Word as our guide, we would serve Thee and build Thy Kingdom upon the earth."

Amidst our prayers, we hear curses as the common sailors brave the freezing torrents, struggling to save the ship. Suddenly a light glows and grows in my mind—I realize that action itself can be a form of prayer, a way of expressing both hope and sincere faith. The moment my father says, "Amen," I jump up at his side and cry out to the other young people in the huddle:

"Let's take heart now and give them a hand topside—show God our willingness to work to survive and build His Church in the new land.

Come—every one of you who can pull a rope and furl a sail!"

A dozen young men and even several elders follow me up on the freezing deck out into the night. Alongside the sailors, we slip and slide and haul in and furl the canvass and struggle until all is battened down and the ship is snug and secure as it can be. And then—the mast does not snap; the keel does not crack; by morning the storm subsides. In a few days, under bright sunshine, we cheer from the open deck as the new shore rises to sight. We give thanks to Him who has seen our struggle and has brought us through.

Eagerly we disembark and hold services. Soon I help my parents stake and clear their land, raise up their cabin of logs, get the first crops planted, and tend them through to harvest. Then we all congregate, even the Indians who have more helped than hindered us, for a feast of grateful thanksgiving.

But what is this? The English lords still will not leave us alone? As Boston grows nearby, its harbor fills with redcoats, domineering over us settlers, laughing at our rough clothes and idealistic compacts and declarations of free conscience under God. My course becomes increasingly clear; finally I announce my fateful choice:

"Dear Father and Mother, I must leave you now, content that you can carry on, but certain also that life will never be what it should, however hard we labor, until the yoke of oppression is overthrown. Yes, I have enlisted on the patriots' side. I will be drilling with the others at night away from here, for the hour in which we rise up is near to hand."

My mother cries, my father dubiously shakes his head, but then they clap me on the back and clasp my hand and bless me and beg God's mercy that I may succeed. Into the night I ride, rounding the outskirts of the town as the signaling candlelights blink in the church tower. The tinkling sounds of redcoat revelry reach my ears. By morning we have assembled undetected on the hill. At last our cannon erupt to announce our declaration. As the British scramble under the bombardment to sober themselves and find arms, we march forward, the bright fife sounding in our ears and the drum giving voice to the heavy beating of our hearts. I see the enemy stumbling to form lines. I hear the order, I stop, I stand and fire. I see them fall, and then we are together, locked in mortal combat hand-to-hand. I feel caught up in a swirl of steel and smoke; but when it is over, I see we are triumphant over a field of red. I release my grip and look at the man I have killed—some older, bleary eyed veteran of many wars, a mercenary, the very same who on the wharf in Boston had pushed me with a contemptuous laugh, threatening that I'd "better move along." How pathetically plain he looks now. Just a fellow human who might have been a friend.

I bear now within myself the only martial decoration that really matters—confidence in one's own courage, proven by one's firmness in the fray. Joyously, I return to reassure my parents, then declare my desire to make the most of a free man's opportunity in a triumphant new country. Singing in my heart, I go back up to Boston to seek an education from the college there. I take up both science and divinity—but then I discover a new obstacle. For all my brilliance in recitation, the fine young sons of the well-to-do with their handsome manners make fun of me. Also, the great city is more costly than I had supposed. I must black the boots and carry the baggage of my fellow students to provide myself just the necessities of life. At times I grow dizzy and cannot concentrate. The professor squints at me from his podium:

"I say there, are you well? The answer you have given is excellent, but it has nothing to do with the question I asked."

Loud male voices, from throats warmed by immaculate, white linen collars, erupt with the hard laughter of scorn. Some of it comes from those Southern aristocrats who never study as I do but who treat me as if I were one of their slaves.

However, there is also now the dear girl I love, she who welcomes me to her father's huge house on the Hill, she who encourages my mind and responds to my verses with her own. But how can I subject her to the shame I bear? Every dandy I serve at college comes also to court this radiant maiden. Certainly I dare not speak to her father, the chief magistrate, before I have something more than poverty to present. I struggle on; I black the boots and eat the crusts of bread and study and recite until neither the professors nor my classmates can deny what I have achieved. At last my diploma is bestowed in the grand ceremony that she, elegant and proud and smiling, comes to attend; to my cheek alone does she give a quick, encouraging kiss of congratulation. I march straightaway to her house and resolutely seek the long-anticipated audience. To her formidable father I make my plea for her hand.

"Oh my dear fellow," is his kindly response, "you are welcome to continue visiting here, of course. Such a smart young lad. But you surely recognize how impossible your request must be. Your family has only a dirt farm, I believe you said? You have nothing but that piece of the college's fine paper with which to maintain my daughter's proper station? Please, please—you have surely learned more than to suppose I could sanction such a prospect for her. But come—let me help you just the same. As a matter of fact, one of my warehouses needs right now a clerk who can write and do sums."

I rush from the great house in anguish, bitterness, and shame. I send her whom I adore, and will adore forever, a farewell message. I give her no chance to respond with charitable comfort or hope: "Dear lady, I release you from a love that can now be but a burden." In twenty-four hours I depart with only a gun and some food in my saddlebag, headed for I know not where in the illimitable reaches of the newly opened West.

Such a bustle on the great rivers! By ferry and flatboat I make my way to civilization's very edge, astonished at the variety of crude humanity I see from all over the globe, pushing and shoving along the westering way. But at last I outdistance them all and find the solitude I need in an unfettered atmosphere. The crackling quiet of the tiny campfire; the huge and silent forests, ancient and virginal; the high rims of the magnificent canyons; the murmuring laughter of the tumbling falls; the great ranges of snow-capped mountains that call me onward in my intrepid quest to the very peaks among the clouds. Yes, here alone is solace for the bruised heart and freedom for the spirit and mind.

One night I awake with a start from my half-sleep; have I been discovered? But no, my horse would have alerted me if there were worse than a real owl behind the owl-like sounds, and he, my companion of the trail, is grazing by the stream below. I relax my grip on the gun that I have learned to use with unfailing accuracy. But there are nights when I narrowly escape the pursuing Ute and the sharp-eyed Cheyenne, my independence underscored by constant exposure to peril. Every so often, I gather my pelts, sew up into my coat the gold I have panned, and break camp, sensing it is time to move on again, for vigilance is truly freedom's price, as even the night owl knows.

In the spring I descend to the wide, green valley where the shallow rivers meet and the traders have their fort of wood-post walls. Among others I meet there is a Sioux chief, who with his family has come to trade. His beautiful dusky daughter eyes me shyly. But some restless thing within tells me that I must move on. Am I ready to confront civilization again? Beyond is the prairie, where I find tiny, dusty towns, full of frontiersmen of every kind. In their several saloons, whiskey flows freely, and loose women openly offer their favors for pay. Laughing, fringe-coated men dance to the sounds of harmonicas and old fiddles. Continuous gambling games attract the unwary, and every day has its more dangerous diversions—a sudden fight with fists or knives or guns, a robbery, a murder, a duel. Life is on the loose out here, and one need care only about one's own.

Then one day I see a blue-coated man ride in, dusty but still eye-stoppingly splendid in bright sabre and sharp spurs and golden epaulets. He signals that he would speak:

"Boys, listen to me—just quiet for a spell. Boys, your country is coming apart. Rebels have arisen and may be striking even tonight at the homes you have left behind. I'm here to recruit a regiment, boys, of the best men on Earth with horse and gun. Who'll rally to the colors and ride beside me against the Rebs? Come on now—who'll join?!"

My blood stirs; without a thought I arise. So then do many others.

Once again it is almost morning. Ears back and alert, our horses are full of fear, sensing that something is coming. They snort, paw in the damp grass, and thrash their tails against the mosquito droves. Mounted, we sweat in our heavy blue uniforms, uncomfortable in the humid night air of lowland Virginia. We inspect our pistols for the third or fourth time; we check our sabres again and again. Somewhere over the gray-green hill, the Rebs are crouching, waiting, not certain from whence we will come, but suspecting that the dawn will bring us.

Light suddenly makes a gold rim of the horizon and burnishes the hills. The trumpet erupts, and then all is snorting horses and jangling bridles and creaking saddles and the thundering sounds of hooves as finally we burst out from the woods that fringe the hill's north slope. Shouting wildly, we near the hilltop at full charge before the Rebs can react. Once they do, their cannon balls rip swaths through our ranks, and minié balls whistle past our ears or thud thickly into the flesh of our comrades and friends. But it is too late; we are too many and galloping too fast. We break into their lines with pistol-shot and sabre-stroke. Our wheeling animals strike foot soldiers to the ground and scatter artillery batteries. I empty both my pistols, and my sabre blade drips bright red as a dozen gray coats go down around my horse's feet. Suddenly—a blast at short range—oh God, I too am falling! I lie then on the ground, but I feel light of heart as the darkening of my wound closes over me, for I know that we have won. We have done our duty, turned the crucial flank, and made the rebels run.

I awake in a field hospital, and convalesce there until at last I hear the beautiful words: "You are going home." The train takes me there with other veterans of the now-concluded war. With them I hobble off on my crutches—all the bands of Boston are lined up to lead us in. Cheers greet us and confetti flies. It is the chief magistrate himself—my true love's now-relenting father—who pins the decorations on our breasts. Whispering to me privately, he asks if I can be forgiving, and tells me that she loves me still, if I still care.

"You are alive and the nation is safe!" she cries, throwing her arms about my neck and sobbing on my shoulder for joy. At the sumptuous welcome banquet, where nothing is denied that her father can afford and my own parents are accorded places of honor, he speaks of the future that peace will now make possible—and, to me, of the need for educated men who have also seen the waiting West.

"If you will yet become my son," he declares, "we will seize these opportunities together, and then you will also be my heir."

After our marriage and long honeymoon—oh, perfect days so sweetly spent by the Great Falls!—I set out with my father-in-law's blessing in his firm's special railroad car, once again heading across the Alleghenies. Under the pitiless western sun, I chart the routes and direct the crews that bring the railroad closer to completion. In the thin air of the mountains, I locate the rich lodes and organize mines. In the heat of the dry prairies, I establish ranches and drive the rustlers away. In the freezing northern snows, I set up lumber mills and lead the cutting of immense forests. In the destitute South, I bring inventions that make crops profitable and launch steam riverboats for marketing. And at each year's end, I return to the eastern investment offices. With glasses of New Year's cheer standing on our mantel, I lead the firm's officers in summing up what our sweat and strength, our vision and risk-taking, our ingenuity and efficiency, have won.

In the tender times away from work—oh, sweet holidays!—my wife and I bundle the children into the sleigh. Pulled by the old bays, bigger than the ponies they love to ride in summer, we sing and jingle through the snow until we arrive at the gate at grandmother's. She and grandfather are retired on the old farm now, but they still keep some chickens for fresh eggs and collie dogs and woolly lambs for the grandchildren when they come. We hug and kiss each other and find presents under the Christmas tree.

One day, our joy is interrupted by the death of my dear father-in-law. Now I must head up the home office, accept the presidency of the entire firm. First my dear darling and I need to get away in our grief. I take her to Paris and Vienna and Rome. In the great art galleries and concert halls, we restore our spirits; but what a backward place Old Europe is. Full of counts and even kings, but one afternoon it comes to me as we sit in a sidewalk cafe after a morning at the Eiffel Tower—here are no real entrepreneurs. And these old hotels, these homes—so uncomfortable and difficult and out-of-date. What a market for ingenious Americans.

Back home and in charge, I plan the expansion of our operations overseas. I buy whole companies, combine them in conglomerates, race to reach new markets and open them ahead of competitors. But what is this? The Old World and its wicked ways still frustrate us. Out of Germany it comes, this spreading cancer, this militaristic sickness that soon enmeshes all of Europe in a war.

I who have seen it coming must alert my fellow citizens who have not crossed the ocean from Fortress America. I must stand for public office, seek election to the Senate as the great foreign-policy forum from which to promulgate my message, to keep America out of the European entanglement if possible, but if not, to enter the fray in full force, wage war determined to win, and make the world safe again.

We do win, and when at last it is over and our boys are coming home, I long to "come home" as well, to relinquish public responsibility. My party presses me: "Only you can reunite the nation as president; only you can lead us to prosperity in peace. Please say you'll run!" But I am no self-seeking politician, dependent on the adulation of fickle crowds; I cherish my own fireside. I fend off the effort to draft me, accept elevation only to the chairmanship of my company's board, and devote myself to domestic duty and pleasure. Each night back in the city, I wave to neighbors from the window of my automobile on my way home from the Stock Exchange or the Civic Board. I drive through the quiet suburban streets lined by leafy trees, handsome brick houses, and gabled bungalows. At home I survey with satisfaction the close-cropped lawn, the solid oaks, the flowers, and the trimmed hedges. I step expectantly across the wide porch and into the front hall, where my dear kisses my cheek as she takes my hat and coat and tells me how long until dinner. In the living room, the children sit at my knee to seek my help with their homework. Then, in my slippers, I light my pipe, pick up the evening paper, and turn on the radio. Jazz music, Jack Benny, baseball scores—but what is it also saying? Something about bread lines, Berlin, bombs?

What a frustration, the world we must deal with abroad! Even at the movies the newsreels are replete with strutting Nazis and arrogant Japanese, while our own economy crashes. This time let there be no hesitation. I accept a call into the Cabinet to preside over arms production. I mobilize the industrial might that I myself have helped develop; I know that our technology will be triumphant. And soon it is, in the hands of our brave sons, my eldest included, although he comes home on a stretcher from someplace called Iwo Jima. The endless days and nights of wartime effort take their toll on me as well. On the day of victory, something in my chest gives way. They rush me to the hospital to arrest the heart attack. There he is too, my soldier son. "Father," he says, "I pray God that you will survive—together we can build a new world of peace and prosperity." Encouraged by one another, we vow neither to succumb.

The magic of medical science restores us both. I then prepare him to take over from me the reins of our multinational industrial and commercial firms. My wife and I wave the other children off to college, confident that they will carry on with cancer curing, atom splitting, and computer solutions for all. Taking our retirement on Florida's warm shore, we fish a little, play golf and bridge, and watch the football games on weekend afternoons. Television tells us of developments that puzzle us—Korea, Vietnam, men walking on the moon—but we can't give in to communism, of course. And the baby boom, as they call it, we readily understand. We are surrounded now with darling grandchildren. My old dear and I raise the flag as always on July 4, hold hands in the gathering twilight as the fireworks fly, and confidently compose our souls to meet our Maker on the Judgment Day. God Bless America. Amen.

PERMISSIONS

Several essays in this book originally appeared as articles in magazines or journals. The author is grateful for permission to reprint them, as follows:

"Ten Strange Ways to Celebrate a Centennial" is reprinted, in revised form, by permission of the publisher, from Gerald George, "Ten Strange Ways to Celebrate a Centennial," *History News*, Volume 43, Number 5 (September/October 1988): 23-25. Copyright © 1988 by the American Association for State and Local History.

"The Ghosts of Drayton Hall" is reprinted, in revised form, by permission of the publisher, from Gerald George, "The Great Drayton Hall Debate," *History News*, Volume 39, Number 1 (January 1984): 7-12. Copyright © 1984 by the American Association for State and Local History.

"Are We Seeing Any History Yet?" is reprinted, in revised form, by permission of the publisher, from Gerald George, review of *Past Meets Present*, ed. Jo Blatti, *History News*, Volume 42, Number 6 (November/December 1987): 28-29. Copyright © 1987 by the American Association for State and Local History.

"The Rise and Fall of Cairo, Illinois" is a revision of an article that first appeared in *Chicago History*, Volume XIV, Number 2 (Summer 1985): 38-49, and is reproduced by permission. Copyright © 1985 by the Chicago Historical Society.

"Learning from Lester" is a revision of an article that first appeared in *The Public Historian*, Volume 7, Number 4 (Fall 1985): 65-70, and is reproduced by permission. Copyright © 1985 by the Regents of the University of California.

"If Ben Franklin Had Known About Texas" is a revision of an article that first appeared in *Federation Reports*, Volume VII, Number 6 (Nov./Dec. 1984): 4-6, and is reproduced by permission of the National Federation of State Humanities Councils.

"The Virgin's Lift" (in the essay "Great Historians I Have Known") first appeared as part of an article on the Chicago Art Institute in *Chicago Times* magazine, Volume 1, Number 5 (May/June 1988): 59-65, and is reproduced by permission. Copyright © 1988 by the Chicago Times Company.

"The Best-Laid Plans of Mice and Museums, Observations on Going Astray," is reprinted, in revised form, by permission of the publisher, from Gerald George, "The Best-Laid Plans of Mice and Museums, Observations on Going Astray," *History News*, Volume 44, Number 2 (March/April 1989): 12-15. Copyright © 1989 by the American Association for State and Local History.